Test Prep Guide

to accompany

New Jersey Code of Criminal Justice

Kenneth Del Vecchio, Esq.

PEARSON

Prentice
Hall

Upper Saddle River, New Jersey

Editor-in-Chief: Vernon R. Anthony
Executive Editor: Frank Mortimer, Jr.
Assistant Editor: Mayda Bosco
Editorial Assistant: Jillian Allison
Managing Editor: Mary Carnis
Production Editor: John Shannon/Laserwords
Production Liaison: Brian Hyland/Janice Stangel
Director of Manufacturing and Production: Bruce Johnson
Marketing Manager: Adam Kloza
Manufacturing Buyer: Cathleen Petersen
Manufacturing Manager: Ilene Sanford
Cover Design: Cheryl Asherman
Printer/Binder: OPM Digital Services

Pearson Education LTD.
Pearson Education Singapore, Pte. Ltd
Pearson Education, Canada, Ltd
Pearson Education–Japan

Pearson Education Australia PTY, Limited
Pearson Education North Asia Ltd
Pearson Educaçion de Mexico, S.A. de C.V.
Pearson Education Malaysia, Pte. Ltd

10 9 8 7 6 5 4 3 2 1
ISBN 0-13-243903-4

This book is dedicated to all of the law enforcement officers and criminal attorneys who seek justice in the daily performance of their duties.

About the Author

Kenneth Del Vecchio is a criminal lawyer who has tried nearly 400 cases, serving as both a prosecutor and a defense attorney. He is also a critically acclaimed filmmaker whose movies star multiple Emmy and Academy Award winners and nominees. He is a faculty member at Fairleigh Dickinson University and teaches intensive criminal law seminars to law enforcement officers and attorneys throughout the State of New Jersey. In addition, Mr. Del Vecchio is a published novelist and the founder and chairman of New Jersey's largest film festival, the New Jersey International Film and Screenplay Festival.

As a lawyer, Mr. Del Vecchio is credited with being one of the youngest attorneys in New Jersey history to try and win a felony jury trial. Since then, he has handled literally thousands of criminal cases as both a prosecutor and criminal defense attorney.

Mr. Del Vecchio has served as prosecutor of both the Borough of Hawthorne and the City of Clifton. On the defense side, he represents clients in criminal matters all across New Jersey. He is a member of the New Jersey and Pennsylvania bars, having been admitted to both states in 1994.

Often headlined as a Renaissance Man, Mr. Del Vecchio has been the subject of hundreds of national magazine and newspaper articles. He has been called The Triple Threat: Attorney, Author, Filmmaker by print and television media.

Mr. Del Vecchio's films, primarily focusing on matters of criminal law, include *The Drum Beats Twice, Tinsel Town, Pride & Loyalty,* and *Rules for Men.* His published criminal suspense novels are *Revelation in the Wilderness* and *Pride & Loyalty,* and he has at least three additional criminal law books soon to be published by Prentice Hall.

Mr. Del Vecchio resides in the Borough of North Haledon with his wife Francine.

Contents

Contents

1

Preliminary

1. There is no statute of limitations for which of the following offenses?

   A. murder
   B. aggravated manslaughter
   C. manslaughter
   D. all of the above
   E. none of the above

2. Michael Westmont wore a white handkerchief mask, brandished a sawed-off shotgun, fired shots in the air, and then stole a man's Mercedes. In order to convict Westmont of theft, the prosecution must prove his guilt:

   A. by clear and convincing evidence
   B. by showing probable cause
   C. beyond a reasonable doubt
   D. through expert testimony
   E. through a telescope

3. Rodney Crawson slapped Bill McNichol in the face in the Seventeen Diner in Carlstadt. In order to convict Crawson of simple assault, the prosecution must prove his guilt:

   A. by clear and convincing evidence
   B. by showing probable cause
   C. beyond a reasonable doubt
   D. through expert testimony
   E. through a telescope

4. Bill McNichol met with Michael Westmont in a restaurant in Montclair, New Jersey. At the restaurant meeting, McNichol paid Westmont $10,000 to steal Rodney Crawson's yacht. Westmont then drove to Connecticut where Crawson stored his yacht in a warehouse. There Westmont hitched the yacht to a heavy-duty trailer and sped off. In which state could Westmont be convicted of theft?

   A. Connecticut
   B. New Jersey
   C. New York
   D. a and b
   E. b and c

5. Assume the same facts as above. If Westmont could be convicted of the crime of theft in New Jersey—for stealing the yacht located in Connecticut—which of the following facts allows the New Jersey conviction?

   A. Westmont drove through New Jersey, blowing through tolls, eventually arriving in Connecticut.
   B. Westmont conspired with McNichol in New Jersey to steal the yacht and an overt act in furtherance of the conspiracy—providing a $10,000 payment—occurred in New Jersey.
   C. Westmont is a New Jersey resident.
   D. all of the above
   E. Westmont cannot be convicted of the Connecticut yacht theft in New Jersey.

6. What is the maximum sentence of imprisonment for committing a petty disorderly persons offense?

   A. 10 days
   B. 30 days
   C. 90 days
   D. six months
   E. A person cannot be sentenced to any term of imprisonment for committing a petty disorderly persons offense.

The following fact pattern pertains to Questions 7–9.

In 2003, Lara hit Robert in the arm in front of Officer Wellenheimer of the Norwood Police Department. Robert, in an effort to save his relationship with Lara, pleads with Officer Wellenheimer not to charge Lara with any offense. Two years later, in 2005, Officer Wellenheimer is called to Robert's house on an anonymous tip that Lara smashed Robert's PopTarts against his living room mirror. When Officer Wellenheimer arrived at Robert's home, strawberry paste indeed covered the mirror, and there was a crack in it. Both Robert and Lara deny that Lara cracked the mirror and the entirety of the PopTart incident. Still, Officer Wellenheimer charges Lara for cracking Robert's mirror and for simple assault for hitting Robert in 2003.

7. The simple assault charge:

   A. will succeed because Officer Wellenheimer witnessed the offense
   B. will succeed because hitting someone in the arm amounts to simple assault
   C. will fail because simple assault is a disorderly persons offense, and a prosecution for a disorderly persons offense must commence within one year after it is committed
   D. a and b
   E. none of the above

8. The criminal mischief charge:

    A. will succeed because the smeared strawberry and cracked mirror support the anonymous tip

    B. will succeed because of "modus operendi"

    C. will succeed because it was timely filed

    D. will fail because criminal mischief is a disorderly persons offense and Officer Wellenheimer did not witness the offense

    E. will fail because Robert and Lara are robots

9. If Lara were convicted of the disorderly persons offense of simple assault for hitting Robert in the arm, the maximum term of imprisonment she could receive is:

    A. 30 days

    B. 90 days

    C. six months

    D. one year

    E. five years

10. Generally, per 2C:1-6, prosecutions for crimes must be commenced within _____ years of their commission in order to avoid being barred for failing to meet the statute of limitations.

    A. 2

    B. 5

    C. 10

    D. 15

    E. 20

11. The following offense is a first degree crime:

    A. kidnapping

    B. aggravated sexual assault

    C. murder

    D. all of the above

    E. none of the above

12. North Haledon Police Sergeant Kyle Book charged local thug Bobby Bannister with a fourth degree theft offense for stealing $400 cash from Enzo's Pizza. The maximum term of imprisonment that Bannister faces for this fourth degree charge is:

    A. 30 days
    B. six months
    C. 18 months
    D. three years
    E. 10 years

13. "Offense" means:

    A. a crime
    B. a disorderly persons offense
    C. a petty disorderly persons offense
    D. all of the above
    E. b and c only

14. Crimes are:

    A. offenses for which the potential prison term exceeds six months
    B. divided into four degrees: fourth, third, second, and first
    C. offenses that entitle an individual to a trial by jury
    D. all of the above
    E. none of the above

General Principles of Liability

1. Marcus has an epileptic seizure and involuntarily slaps George in the face, breaking George's nose. Which of the following statements is true?

   A. Marcus can appropriately be charged with simple assault because he caused bodily injury to George.
   B. Marcus can appropriately be charged with simple assault because he was negligent by not removing himself from the company of others once his seizure began.
   C. Marcus should not be charged with simple assault because of the doctrine of merger.
   D. Marcus should not be charged with simple assault because his act of slapping George was involuntary.
   E. Marcus should be charged with aggravated assault.

2. Football star Bill McNichol paid Michael Westmont to commit an armed robbery. Westmont, draped in a white handkerchief and brandishing a sawed-off shotgun, heisted keys from another football player and stole his brand-new Mercedes. Can McNichol be charged with the armed robbery by Michael Westmont even though McNichol did not actually tote the gun or drive off in the Mercedes?

   A. Yes, he is accountable for the robbery as an accomplice because he solicited the offense by arranging it and paying for it to happen.

   B. Yes, he is accountable for the robbery as a conspirator, arranging for the act to occur and paying for it to happen.

   C. Yes, he is accountable for the robbery by the doctrine of merger.

   D. a and b only

   E. b and c only

The following fact pattern pertains to Questions 3 and 4.

A man masked in a white handkerchief beat a jewelry store clerk with a baseball bat. A shirtless, barefoot man accompanied the masked man and repeatedly screamed, "Knock the dude out!" The shirtless man then stuffed a handful of diamonds in the masked man's pocket. The jewelry clerk, severely beaten, suffered a fractured skull and a broken nose.

3. Should the shirtless man be charged with the armed robbery of the jewelry store?

   A. no, because he never struck the jewelry clerk

   B. no, because he was obviously insane

   C. yes, because he was an accomplice to the offense as he aided the masked man in committing it

   D. yes, because robbery is a first degree crime

   E. c and d only

4. Which of the following defenses could relieve the shirtless man of culpability for the beating of the jewelry clerk?

    A. consent—if the jewelry clerk had agreed to the baseball bat beating
    B. mistake of law—if the shirtless man mistakenly believed that the beating was legal
    C. intoxication—if the shirtless man had been injected with PCP, which was not self-induced and it resulted in his inability to know the nature and quality of his actions
    D. all of the above
    E. none of the above

5. In which of the following situations would the defense of duress most likely succeed for the shirtless man?

    A. The shirtless man joined the masked man in the jewelry store robbery because he was clinically depressed.
    B. The shirtless man smoked a dime bag of hash and didn't understand what was happening at the jewelry store.
    C. The masked man told the shirtless man that they were filming a movie and the whole incident wasn't real.
    D. The shirtless man was in a bad mood.
    E. The shirtless man was forced by gunpoint to join in the robbery.

6. Where is consent to bodily harm *not* a defense?

    A. in a boxing match
    B. if the bodily harm inflicted is serious such as in a stabbing
    C. if the bodily harm inflicted causes a bruised bicep
    D. in a wrestling match
    E. Consent to bodily harm is never a defense.

7. A police officer handcuffed a jewelry store robbery suspect to a pole as he chased a second suspect. One arm was cuffed to the pole while the other was free. The handcuffed suspect had punched the store's clerk in the face and grabbed diamonds before the police officer arrived. Once handcuffed, the suspect began chatting with the jewelry clerk, who was tending to a bruised eye. Suddenly, the suspect reached into his coat pocket. The clerk, alarmed, reached for a gun behind the counter and shot and killed the suspect. Later, it was learned that the suspect was reaching for a hairbrush. Should the jewelry clerk be charged with a homicide offense?

   A. yes, because the suspect was handcuffed to the pole
   B. yes, because the suspect was not armed and was only reaching for a brush
   C. no, because the jewelry clerk made a mistake of fact, reasonably believing that the suspect was reaching for a weapon
   D. no, because the jewelry clerk was under duress
   E. The jewelry clerk should be charged with a contempt offense instead of a homicide offense.

8. The defense of entrapment is unavailable:

   A. when a law enforcement officer is involved
   B. when it is coupled with a drug offense
   C. when the defendant charged perjured himself
   D. when the charged offense involves causing or threatening bodily injury
   E. all of the above

3

General Principles of Justification

1. Jillian Peterson enters a car dealership wielding two machetes. She orders the dealership manager to go to the business's safe and retrieve all the cash in it. The manager complies with her demands and turns over $50,000 to Peterson. As she's about to leave the store, however, Peterson turns around and whips one of the machetes at the manager's head, narrowly missing. The manager then fires two shots at Peterson, instantly killing her. Was the manager justified in using deadly force against Jillian Peterson?

   A. no, because a machete is not a deadly weapon and therefore he was not facing death or serious bodily harm
   B. no, because Peterson may have missed him again if she threw the second machete
   C. yes, because the manager reasonably believed that deadly force was necessary to protect himself against death or serious bodily harm
   D. yes, because the manager was following company policy
   E. a and b only

2. When can deadly force be used in defense of property?

   A. when the property value exceeds $10,000
   B. when the property value exceeds $50,000
   C. when the person reasonably believes that deadly force is necessary to protect the person or another from death or substantial danger of bodily harm
   D. a and c
   E. b and c

3. Under which of the following circumstances would it *not* be justified for a person to use deadly force to protect himself?

   A. if he knows he could retreat from an assailant with complete safety
   B. if he did not reasonably believe that deadly force was necessary to protect himself or another from death or serious bodily harm
   C. if he, with the purpose of causing death or serious bodily harm, provoked the use of force against himself in the same encounter
   D. all of the above
   E. none of the above

4. When may a law enforcement officer use deadly force?

   A. to thwart a kidnapping
   B. to stop an aggravated sexual assault in progress
   C. to stop the theft of a bicycle
   D. a and b only
   E. none of the above

4

Responsibility

1. A defendant may succeed in an insanity defense:

   A. only if two licensed psychiatrists testify at trial that he is legally insane
   B. if he did not know the nature and quality of the act he was doing
   C. if he did know the nature and quality of the act he was doing but did not know what he was doing was wrong
   D. a and b only
   E. b and c only

5

Inchoate Crimes

1. During a robbery of a car dealership, Jillian Peterson whipped a machete at the manager's head, narrowly missing him. Before she threw the machete, she advised that she was going to kill him. Which of the following elements are necessary for Peterson to be charged with attempted murder?

   A. that she took a substantial step in attempting to murder the manager by throwing the machete at his head
   B. that her throwing of the machete was strongly corroborative of her criminal purpose to kill the manager
   C. that she embraced an indicia of belief manifested by one who attempts to engage in criminal conduct
   D. a and b only
   E. a and c only

2. An individual can be convicted of conspiracy if:

    A. he agrees with other person(s) to commit a crime
    B. he steals more than $5,000 but less than $100,000
    C. he engages in *res ipsa loquitor*
    D. all of the above
    E. none of the above

3. Conspiracy to commit a first degree crime generally is:

    A. a first degree crime
    B. a second degree crime
    C. a third degree crime
    D. a fourth degree crime
    E. a disorderly persons offense

4. A person is guilty of manufacturing burglar tools only if:

    A. the tools could also be used as a deadly weapon
    B. the person knows the tools are commonly used for burglary purposes and intends to use the tools, or provide them to others, for use in a burglary
    C. the person knows that the tools are commonly used for burglary purposes and that they could be used as a deadly weapon
    D. the tools are manufactured at a steel factory
    E. none of the above

5. Conspiracy to commit murder is:

    A. a disorderly persons offense
    B. a fourth degree crime
    C. a third degree crime
    D. a second degree crime
    E. a first degree crime

6. Slick Sammy conspires with Charlotte and Neal to steal $5,000 from Big Busts, LLC. The conspiracy charge against Sammy would be:

   A. a disorderly persons offense
   B. a fourth degree crime
   C. a third degree crime
   D. a second degree crime
   E. a first degree crime

7. In order to be convicted of being a leader of organized crime, a defendant must:

   A. purposefully conspire with others as an organizer, supervisor, manager, or financier to commit a continuing series of crimes that constitutes a pattern of racketeering activity
   B. at least recklessly conspire with others as an organizer, supervisor, manager, or financier to commit a continuing series of crimes that constitutes a pattern of racketeering activity
   C. have at least 50 people working under him
   D. a and c only
   E. b and c only

8. Which of the following statements about the crime of conspiracy is *not* true?

   A. In order to convict someone of conspiracy, those involved in the crime(s) must conspire in at least two states in furtherance of the conspiracy.
   B. An overt act in furtherance of the conspiracy is generally required to convict someone of conspiracy.
   C. Generally, one who conspires to commit a number of crimes will be convicted of only one count of conspiracy.
   D. all of the above
   E. none of the above

The following fact pattern pertains to Questions 9 and 10.

Phantom X conspired with Paul, Frank, Mark and 10 others to commit 13 separate robberies. Phantom X organized the group and financed their individual robberies, paying for the weapons and other necessary materials. The New Jersey State Attorney General determined that this series of organized, continuing criminal events constituted a pattern of racketeering activity.

9. Phantom X could be charged with:

    A. maintaining a CDS manufacturing outfit
    B. cleaning, under the Clean Hands doctrine
    C. being a leader of organized crime
    D. being leader of a Contemptuous Illegal Facility
    E. committing attempted contempt

10. Let's say Paul never actually met Phantom X or any of the other individuals who committed robberies for Phantom X's organization. Given this situation, which of the following is true?

    A. Paul could not be charged with conspiracy because he actually never met Phantom X or the others who conspired to commit the robberies.
    B. Paul could not be charged with conspiracy because he did not organize the group.
    C. Paul could not be charged with conspiracy because of the "$100,000 requirement."
    D. all of the above
    E. Paul could be charged with conspiracy even though he never actually met Phantom X or the others who conspired to commit the robberies.

11. An attempt to commit the crime of terrorism is:

    A. a first degree crime
    B. a second degree crime
    C. a third degree crime
    D. a fourth degree crime
    E. a disorderly persons offense

12. Leroy attempts to commit a first degree carjacking. He is caught by Newark Police Officer Lamar Wilkins before he is successful. Leroy's charge of attempted carjacking is:

    A. a first degree crime
    B. a second degree crime
    C. a third degree crime
    D. a fourth degree crime
    E. a disorderly persons offense

7

Registration and Notification of Release of Certain Offenders

1. The conviction of the following offense *cannot* give rise to requiring someone to register as a "sex offender":

   A. aggravated sexual assault
   B. sexual assault
   C. aggravated criminal sexual contact
   D. lewdness
   E. kidnapping

2. Corky was "acquitted by reason of insanity" of luring a 12-year-old child into his automobile where he exposed his genitals to the child. Is Corky required to register as a sex offender?

   A. no, because he was acquitted of the offense by reason of insanity
   B. no, because the crime of luring does not give rise to a requirement for someone to register as a sex offender
   C. no, because the child must be 10 years old or younger
   D. no, because of the "Affirmative Defense Doctrine"
   E. Yes, Corky must register as a sex offender

3. Failing to register as a sex offender is:

   A. a crime of the first degree
   B. a crime of the second degree
   C. a crime of the third degree
   D. a crime of the fourth degree
   E. a disorderly persons offense

4. At age 15, Bubba was adjudicated delinquent of sexually assaulting a female. Does Bubba have to register as a sex offender?

   A. yes
   B. no
   C. maybe, depending upon the age of the female
   D. maybe, depending upon Bubba's IQ
   E. maybe, depending upon the judge's recommendation

5. Which statement best describes "adjudicated delinquent"?

   A. a defendant being found liable in small claims court
   B. a court finding that the state has probable cause in a case
   C. a power of attorney
   D. a juvenile found guilty in juvenile court
   E. an adult being stopped for speeding

11

Criminal Homicide

1. Which of the following offenses is *not* a homicide offense as defined in Chapter 11 of Title 2C?

   A. aggravated manslaughter
   B. wrongful death
   C. murder
   D. manslaughter
   E. death by auto

2. In a Hackensack bar, Larry Kelleher argued with George Carmichael over who was next in line for a drink. A fight ensued, which ended with Kelleher physically beating Carmichael to death. Witnesses told police that Kelleher threw the first punch. What would be the most appropriate offense with which to charge Kelleher with?

   A. murder
   B. aggravated manslaughter
   C. manslaughter
   D. aggravated assault
   E. no offense, because Kelleher probably didn't intend to kill Carmichael

3. Let's assume the facts in Question 2 were modified to the following extent. Kelleher, instead of punching Carmichael, went home. After stewing about the bar argument for three days, Kelleher planned a knife attack against Carmichael. On the fourth day, Kelleher waited outside Carmichael's house and then stabbed the man to death as he tried to enter his car. What is the most appropriate offense to charge Kelleher with under these circumstances?

A. murder
B. aggravated manslaughter
C. manslaughter
D. aggravated assault
E. no offense, because Carmichael cut the line

4. The primary difference between aggravated manslaughter and manslaughter is this:

A. Manslaughter simply requires that the defendant cause a death while acting recklessly, but aggravated manslaughter requires that the reckless actions occur under circumstances manifesting extreme indifference to human life.
B. Manslaughter requires that the defendant act with the *mens rea* of negligence, but aggravated manslaughter requires that the defendant act with the *mens rea* of recklessness.
C. The maximum term of imprisonment for manslaughter is 5 years, whereas the maximum term of imprisonment for aggravated manslaughter is 10 years.
D. a and c
E. b and c

5. Brigitte Madison poisoned her brother, an attorney, with several high doses of arsenic. The attorney died from the poisoning, and Madison was the beneficiary of all of his earthly belongings, including a lucrative life insurance policy. Diary entries, hair strands, and fingerprints all indicated that she did indeed intend to poison the man. Further investigation showed that Madison was once previously charged with murder but was acquitted by a jury. Cherry Hill Police charged her with the murder of her brother. What is the best rationale for this charge?

A. Brigitte Madison's previous murder charge showed she had propensity to kill again.

B. It falls under the felony murder component of the murder statute.

C. The evidence indicates that Madison acted with a purposeful intent to cause her brother's death.

D. Usually the appropriate charge would be aggravated manslaughter under these circumstances, but killing an attorney automatically elevates the offense to murder.

E. all of the above

6. Assume that the above facts were modified to the extent that Madison, while cooking soup for her brother, accidentally spilled arsenic in the broth. Aware that the arsenic was in the soup, she still served him the soup. The brother thereafter died from arsenic poisoning. What would be the most appropriate offense for which the Cherry Hill Police to charge Madison?

A. murder, because she was previously charged and acquitted of murder

B. murder, because she planned the killing

C. manslaughter, because she acted negligently in causing her brother's death

D. manslaughter, because she slaughtered a man

E. aggravated manslaughter, because she acted with extreme indifference to human life while recklessly causing her brother's death

7. Manslaughter is:

   A. a first degree crime
   B. a second degree crime
   C. a third degree crime
   D. a fourth degree crime
   E. a disorderly persons offense

8. Which of the following circumstances best describes a felony murder?

   A. William breaks into Beth's house with the intent to kill her. Once inside, he shoots her to death.
   B. Michael keeps a baseball bat in his car. During a road rage incident, he stops at a red light, exits his car, and proceeds to the car in front of him. Once there, he pulls the other driver from his vehicle and beats him to death with the baseball bat.
   C. Jeff Weiss points a pistol at a toll collector in an attempt to rob the man. The toll collector complies and turns over the funds to him. Weiss then flees the scene, with a state trooper chasing him. Attempting to cross from the left lane into the right lane, Weiss loses control of his vehicle and crashes his vehicle into a stranded motorist, killing him instantly.
   D. Barbara shakes her child, ultimately killing the infant.
   E. A corrections officer shot an inmate who was attempting to escape from the jail. The inmate died at the scene.

9. Which of the following best describes a first degree "vehicular homicide" offense:

   A. Jeff, angry at his sister, rushes out of his house completely sober. Not paying attention, he drives the wrong way down a one-way street. Aware that he is driving in the wrong direction, he determines not to stop because he believes no other automobiles will come his way. Suddenly, a pickup truck turns into his path. The crash results in the other driver's death.

   B. Driving on the revoked list and while intoxicated, Jeff races on Route 80 West at over 100 m.p.h. He strikes another vehicle, causing the death of Wilma.

   C. Driving while intoxicated, Jeff accidentally crosses onto a horse farm and kills Bobberino, an animal lover, who was petting his horse, Carmella.

   D. After smoking pot, Jeff drove his 1990 Honda Accord into a factory wall, instantly killing the passenger in his car, Moses.

   E. Driving while intoxicated, Jeff drove the wrong way down a one-way street through a school zone. There, he crashed into a cucumber stand located on the sidewalk. The cucumber salesman, Malanga, was instantly killed by the impact.

10. Aiding another's suicide is:

    A. not a crime under Title 2C
    B. a disorderly persons offense
    C. a third degree offense
    D. a second degree offense
    E. a first degree offense

11. In order to be convicted of a criminal offense for leaving the scene of a motor vehicle accident that results in death, the actor must:

    A. negligently cause the accident
    B. recklessly leave the scene of the accident
    C. knowingly leave the scene of the accident
    D. purposely cause the accident
    E. none of the above

12. Which of the following offenses *cannot* give rise to a felony murder charge?

    A. criminal escape
    B. criminal sexual contact
    C. burglary
    D. kidnapping
    E. carjacking

13. Which homicide offense has a "heat of passion" provision?

    A. aiding suicide
    B. aggravated manslaughter
    C. manslaughter
    D. murder
    E. none of the above

14. What defines the required mental state, or *mens rea,* that an actor must possess in order to be convicted of murder?

    A. The actor purposely causes death or serious bodily injury resulting in death.
    B. The actor knowingly causes death or serious bodily injury resulting in death.
    C. The actor recklessly causes death or serious bodily injury resulting in death.
    D. a and b
    E. a and c

15. Connor repeatedly beats Harley in the head with a gold brick, knocking Harley unconscious. Harley remains in a coma for eight months and then perishes. Which of the following is the best offense with which to charge Connor?

    A. aggravated assault
    B. attempted murder
    C. murder
    D. wrongful death
    E. harassment

The following fact pattern pertains to Questions 16 and 17.

Elliot Rodman and Beef Norton determine to rob a Bloomfield liquor store. Both men, armed with shotguns, enter the liquor store and immediately proceed to the clerk. Elliot and Beef point their shotguns at the clerk's head and demand all of the store's cash. Suddenly, a patron, holding a knife, begins to charge Elliot and Beef in an effort to thwart the robbery. Elliot turns his gun at the patron and shoots and kills him. A moment later, the clerk grabs a pistol he had hidden in his waist and shoots and kills Elliot. At that, Bloomfield police burst through the front door and arrest Beef, who does not put up a struggle.

16. Could Beef be charged with murder for the shooting death of the patron?

    A. Yes, under the felony murder component of the murder statute, Beef is guilty of murder because the death of the patron occurred while he was involved in committing a robbery.
    B. No, because even though a death occurred while Beef was involved in committing a robbery, the offense of robbery is not one of the enumerated crimes that invokes a felony murder charge.
    C. no, because Beef himself did not shoot the patron, nor did he plan or know that Elliot was going to shoot him
    D. no, because the patron was the initial aggressor against Elliot, and Elliot was acting in self-defense
    E. no, because Beef didn't struggle with the police

17. Could Beef be charged with murder for the shooting death of his partner, Elliot?

   A. Yes, under the felony murder component of the murder statute, Beef is guilty of murder because the death of his partner occurred while he was involved in committing a robbery.

   B. No, because even though a death occurred while Beef was involved in committing a robbery, the offense of robbery is not one of the enumerated crimes that invokes a felony murder charge.

   C. no, because the initial aggression of the patron caused the robbery to go awry, which in turn caused the clerk to shoot Elliot

   D. no, because the "accomplice exception" of the felony murder statute relieves Beef of culpability for the deaths of other participants in a crime

   E. no, because Beef didn't struggle with the police

18. Big Ed shoplifted 25 packs of batteries from a supermarket in Maywood. He fled on a motorcycle but was immediately spotted by police. A chase ensued, with Big Ed attempting to elude the police for over a mile. It ended abruptly, however, when Big Ed crashed into a pedestrian, instantly killing the man. For the pedestrian's death, Big Ed should be charged with which of the following offenses?

   A. murder
   B. aggravated manslaughter
   C. manslaughter
   D. wrongful death
   E. felony murder

19. Marge was very ill and constantly in pain. She was unable to walk and care for herself. Marge asked her sister Bethany to assist her in committing suicide. Bethany, troubled by her sister's condition, complied and gave Marge herbal tea with a lethal dose of poison in it. What is the most appropriate offense for which law enforcement to charge Bethany with?

    A. murder
    B. aggravated manslaughter
    C. manslaughter
    D. aiding suicide
    E. no offense because Marge actually carried out
        her suicide by drinking the tea

20. Smalls knows that Lorenzo wants to die because he was just dumped by his girlfriend. In an effort to help Lorenzo obtain his wish, Smalls shoots Lorenzo in the head, killing him instantly. The *best* crime with which to charge Smalls is:

    A. aiding suicide
    B. manslaughter because the killing was in the
        heat of passion
    C. manslaughter because the killing was reckless
    D. murder
    E. none of the above

21. Snooch decides to race against Marlboro Man on Route 15. Both vehicles exceed 100 m.p.h. Snooch, though, loses control of his car and crashes into an oncoming motorist, killing the driver. Snooch should be charged with what offense?

    A. vehicular homicide
    B. knowingly leaving the scene of a motor vehi-
        cle accident resulting in death if he exited his
        vehicle
    C. murder
    D. all of the above
    E. a and b only

22. A person can be charged with murder if he:

    A. purposely kills someone
    B. knowingly causes death to someone
    C. knowingly causes serious bodily injury to someone that results in death
    D. all of the above
    E. a and b only

23. Which of the following *best* describes an aggravated manslaughter?

    A. Crumb Bun forces Mello Yellow to the ground and chops Mello's head off with a machete.
    B. While raping Suzie in the bathtub, Crumb Bun accidentally kills her, electrocuting her when a radio falls in the tub.
    C. Crumb Bun launches a five-ton wrecking ball into a one-family house, aware that Mr. Jingles is inside. Mr. Jingles is killed when the wrecking ball strikes him in the head.
    D. Crumb Bun is attacked by a pack of wolves and their owner, Slapstick. While warding off Slapstick and the wolves with a nightstick, he strikes and kills Slapstick.
    E. Crumb Bun, carrying out a contract, shoots and kills Marmalade.

24. Which of the following *best* describes an act of negligent homicide?

    A. Otis, slipping on a banana peel, falls into Harmon, causing Harmon to fall on the ground and die.
    B. Otis throws a dart into a crowd of drunk bartenders, hitting one of the bartenders in the head. The dart wound gets infected and the bartender dies three months later.
    C. Otis robs a car salesman and kills him when his gun accidentally goes off.
    D. all of the above
    E. none of the above because there is no such thing as negligent homicide

25. A person can be convicted of aiding suicide if:

    A. he negligently aids another to commit suicide and his conduct indeed causes such suicide
    B. he recklessly aids another to commit suicide and his conduct indeed causes such suicide
    C. he purposely aids another to commit suicide and his conduct indeed causes such suicide
    D. all of the above
    E. none of the above

Assault; Reckless Endangering; Threats

1. At a bar, Carley slapped Melissa in the face, causing a scratch on Melissa's face. What is the best offense with which to charge Carley?

   A. harassment
   B. simple assault
   C. aggravated assault
   D. disorderly conduct
   E. luring

The following fact pattern pertains to Questions 2 and 3.

Lance Jones and his brother, Stanley, physically beat a grocer with a set of golf clubs, knocking him unconscious. The grocer's injuries necessitated 40 stitches to his head, and he suffered broken ribs. Newark Police Sergeant Samuel Paterson arrived at the scene, and Lance Jones immediately aimed a pistol at the officer. As he did so, a red laser beam raced from the gun's barrel toward the sergeant's head. The two Jones brothers then fled the scene, with Sergeant Paterson following them.

2. For pointing a firearm at Newark Police Sergeant Samuel Paterson, Lance Jones is guilty of:

   A. disorderly conduct
   B. simple assault
   C. third degree aggravated assault
   D. fourth degree aggravated assault
   E. nothing, because no harm was done to the officer

3. If Samuel Paterson was *not* a police officer but instead a regular citizen, Lance Jones would be guilty of what offense for pointing a firearm at him?

   A. disorderly conduct
   B. simple assault
   C. third degree aggravated assault
   D. fourth degree aggravated assault
   E. nothing, because no harm was done to the person

4. For their golf club beating of the grocery clerk, what is the *most appropriate* offense with which the Jones brothers should be charged?

   A. simple assault
   B. second degree aggravated assault
   C. third degree aggravated assault
   D. fourth degree aggravated assault
   E. attempted murder

5. For pointing at firearm at Sergeant Paterson—that activated a red laser beam, which ran to the officer's head—Lance Jones should be charged with what offense?

   A. an additional charge of simple assault
   B. an additional charge of harassment
   C. an additional charge of disorderly conduct
   D. an additional charge of aggravated assault
   E. nothing, because Jones would already be charged with an offense for pointing the firearm at Sergeant Paterson

6. Terroristic threat is:

   A. a crime of the third degree
   B. a crime of the fourth degree
   C. a disorderly persons offense
   D. a petty disorderly persons offense
   E. any of the above

7. Disarming a law enforcement officer is:

   A. a crime of the first degree if the defendant discharges the firearm
   B. a crime of the second degree if the defendant doesn't discharge the firearm
   C. a crime of the first degree if the defendant threatens to use the firearm against the officer
   D. a crime of the first degree if the officer suffers serious bodily injury once the firearm is disarmed from the officer
   E. all of the above

8. Seaside Heights Police Officer Ronald Queene responds to a call at the Village Night Club. Once there, he encounters Carley, who is screaming at her friend Bob. Carley turns to Officer Queene and slaps him in the face, causing a scratch on the officer's cheek. Under these circumstances, what is the most serious offense of which Carley could be convicted?

   A. third degree aggravated assault
   B. simple assault
   C. disorderly conduct
   D. harassment
   E. nothing, because Officer Queene can deal with it

9. Assume the same facts as above except that Carley slaps Judge Wookey. What is the most serious offense of which Carley could be convicted?

   A. third degree aggravated assault
   B. simple assault
   C. disorderly conduct
   D. harassment
   E. nothing, because Judge Wookey had the bench in front of him and therefore is completely negligent for letting Carley get to him

10. The Jones brothers beat a grocer with golf clubs, leaving him unconscious and causing head injuries that resulted in 40 stitches. Also, the grocer suffered broken ribs from the attack. Thereafter, the Jones brothers fled the scene, leaving the grocer with his injuries. Other than an assault charge, which of the following offenses could the Jones brothers be charged with pertaining to the grocer?

   A. leaving the scene of the accident
   B. obstructing justice
   C. endangering an injured victim
   D. contempt
   E. all of the above

11. The Hawthorne Bears battle it out in a close game with Queen of Peace's Golden Griffiths. Just after Queen of Peace tight end Nick Bender scores a touchdown, 40-year-old Hawthorne dad Terry Timly punches Queen of Peace dad Eddie Kole in the gut. They scuffle, and then Hawthorne Police intervene. What is the most serious offense of which Terry Timly could be convicted?

   A. harassment
   B. disorderly conduct
   C. riot
   D. simple assault
   E. fourth degree aggravated assault

12. Which of the following mental states could give rise to an aggravated assault charge?

    A. acting purposely
    B. acting knowingly
    C. acting recklessly
    D. all of the above
    E. none of the above

13. Toni Gahbuoye is a prisoner of Trenton State Prison, having been convicted of various crimes. Angry at one of the corrections officers, he throws his own sperm at the man. Gahbuoye is guilty of what offense?

    A. aggravated assault
    B. simple assault
    C. disorderly conduct
    D. harassment
    E. improper conduct

14. Throwing bodily fluid at a law enforcement officer is:

    A. a crime of the third degree if the officer suffers bodily injury
    B. a crime of the fourth degree if the officer doesn't suffer bodily injury
    C. always a disorderly persons offense
    D. a and b only
    E. none of the above

15. Which of the following characterizes a difference between simple assault and aggravated assault?

  A. Simple assault requires "significant bodily injury," while aggravated assault requires "serious bodily injury."
  B. Simple assault is a disorderly persons offense, while aggravated assault is a crime.
  C. Simple assault involves only foul language, while aggravated assault requires bodily injury.
  D. Simple assault is a common law crime, while aggravated assault was created by case law.
  E. all of the above

16. Stanley Jones laced his ex-girlfriend's beer with an intoxicating drug that caused her to become tranquilized and disoriented. Thereafter, he sexually assaulted her. Stanley Jones should be charged with which of the following offenses?

  A. simple assault
  B. harassment
  C. disorderly conduct
  D. attempted murder
  E. reckless endangerment

17. Martin and Jeff are playing ping-pong. The game is heated and close. Finally, the score is tied at 20–20. Just before Martin prepares to serve the next ball, he yells over to Jeff, "I'll kill you if you beat me again." Police Officer Kinard overhears what Martin said. With what offense should he charge Martin?

  A. attempted murder
  B. attempted aggravated assault
  C. harassment
  D. terroristic threats
  E. nothing, because Jeff would not reasonably believe that the threat to kill him would likely be carried out

18. The following is an example of a third degree aggravated assault:

    A. Ruppert purposely strikes Bob with a hammer, a deadly weapon, causing "bodily injury" but not "serious bodily injury" to Bob's kneecap.
    B. Ruppert wildly swings a hammer near Bob in an attempt to scare Bob. Ruppert's reckless actions resulted in the hammer striking Bob in the knee, causing Bob "bodily injury" but not "serious bodily injury."
    C. Ruppert purposely shoots Bob in the chest with a .22 caliber pistol.
    D. Ruppert purposely scratches Bob's arm with his fingernail.
    E. all of the above

19. Lance Jones disarmed a uniformed police officer, taking the officer's nightstick from him. Jones's action constitutes:

    A. a petty disorderly persons offense
    B. a disorderly persons offense
    C. a crime of the second degree
    D. an act of arson
    E. a violation of the doctrine of liberalism

20. Thelma purposely shot Louise three times in the head, instantly killing Louise. Thelma should be charged with what offense?

    A. arson
    B. harassment
    C. disorderly conduct
    D. murder
    E. disobedience

21. Stanley Jones repeatedly sat in front of his ex-girlfriend's house, calling her each time she appeared. On each occasion, he threatened to physically beat her. On three of the events, he waved a baseball bat at her as she looked out the window. Stanley Jones could appropriately be charged with which offense?

    A. attempted murder
    B. stalking
    C. reckless endangerment
    D. endangering a victim
    E. all of the above

22. Pointing an imitation firearm at a law enforcement officer is:

    A. a crime of the first degree
    B. a crime of the third degree
    C. a petty disorderly persons offense
    D. a motor vehicle violation
    E. not an offense at all, because is an imitation firearm

23. Major League baseball star Hank Cooke left professional sports, enrolled in law school, and ultimately became a judge. After court one afternoon, Cooke disarmed Donny Defendant, who was pointing a loaded shotgun at Sheriff Officer Arnie Kamalster. Officer Kamalster then arrested Donny Defendant, and Judge Cooke was proclaimed a hero. What is the most appropriate offense with which to charge Donny Defendant?

    A. attempted murder
    B. fourth degree aggravated assault
    C. third degree aggravated assault
    D. harassment
    E. disorderly conduct

24. Assume the same facts as above but that Donny Defendant pointed the loaded firearm at a civilian. What is the most appropriate offense with which to charge Donny Defendant?

    A. attempted murder
    B. fourth degree aggravated assault
    C. third degree aggravated assault
    D. harassment
    E. disorderly conduct

25. In order to convict someone of stalking, which of the following is necessary?

    A. A kidnapping must occur along with the stalking.
    B. A deadly weapon must be involved.
    C. The victim must have previously notified law enforcement that a perpetrator is bothering the victim.
    D. The defendant's course of conduct must cause a reasonable person to fear bodily injury.
    E. none of the above

26. Rosie is infatuated with Greer, the front man of a local rock band. At every gig, she tries to get his autograph. Greer has repeatedly told her "no." Still, she has approached him at the last seven gigs. Rosie is guilty of what offense?

    A. stalking
    B. terroristic threats
    C. disorderly conduct
    D. domestic violence
    E. no offense at all

27. Stalking is elevated from a fourth degree crime to a third degree crime when:

    A. an actor stalks a victim in violation of an existing court order prohibiting the behavior
    B. an actor commits a second offense of stalking against the same victim
    C. an actor commits the crime of stalking while on parole
    D. all of the above
    E. none of the above because stalking is always a first degree crime

28. In order to convict a person of stalking, which of the following elements must be present?

    A. The acts underlying the stalking must cause a reasonable person to fear bodily injury to himself or a member of his immediate family.
    B. There must be an actual act of physical violence.
    C. There must be an act of aggravated assault or a homicide involved.
    D. The victim must be a blood relative of the actor or a spouse, former spouse, or a person who has had a dating relationship with the actor.
    E. The actor must have a prior criminal history involving the victim.

29. Shady McGrady pummels Jamar McMoose in a professional boxing match. McGrady breaks McMoose's nose in the bout. Shady McGrady should be charged with which offense?

    A. attempted murder
    B. aggravated assault
    C. simple assault
    D. disorderly conduct
    E. no offense at all

30. Stewart waves a baseball bat at Albert because Albert wore Stewart's jeans without his permission. Stewart, whose anger is growing, swings the bat near Albert, purposely missing him but frightening Albert. What is the best offense with which to charge Stewart?

   A. terroristic threats
   B. harassment
   C. disorderly conduct
   D. simple assault
   E. aggravated assault

31. Which of the following does *not* constitute an offense in New Jersey?

   A. pointing a firearm at a police officer
   B. pointing an imitation firearm
   C. pointing a firearm at a civilian
   D. pointing at a police officer
   E. c and d

The following fact pattern pertains to Questions 32 and 33.

Bill yells at Mike to "turn the down the music." Mike, angry at Bill, pushes him. Bill suffers no injuries.

32. What is the *best* offense with which to charge Mike?

   A. aggravated assault
   B. simple assault
   C. harassment
   D. disorderly conduct
   E. no offense at all

33. What is the *best* offense with which to charge Bill?

   A. terroristic threats
   B. harassment
   C. disorderly conduct
   D. riot
   E. no offense at all

Kidnapping and Related Offenses: Coercion

1. Mercury Anderson, 50, enters the automobile of Kung Po, 30. Anderson locks the vehicle's doors and refuses to allow Po to leave the car for approximately 15 minutes. Anderson's actions amount to which offense?

    A. criminal restraint as long as his restraint did not subject Po to a risk of serious bodily injury
    B. false imprisonment as long as his restraint did not subject Po to a risk of serious bodily injury
    C. kidnapping as long as his restraint was not due to a familial relationship
    D. involuntary servitude as long as his restraint was not consensual
    E. all of the above

2. In order to be convicted of criminal coercion:

   A. the defendant must purposefully and unlawfully act to restrict another's freedom of action to engage or refrain from engaging in conduct
   B. the defendant must recklessly and unlawfully act to restrict another's freedom of action to engage or refrain from engaging in conduct
   C. the defendant must purposefully lure the victim to engage in specific conduct
   D. the defendant must, with knowledge, lure the victim to engage in specific conduct
   E. the defendant must coerce the victim into buying a sports-utility vehicle

3. Kidnapping is:

   A. a crime of the third degree only
   B. a crime of the second degree only
   C. a crime of the first degree only
   D. a crime of the first, second, or third degree, depending upon the circumstances
   E. a crime of the first or second degree, depending upon the circumstances

4. "Involuntary servitude" is part of which offense?

   A. criminal restraint
   B. false imprisonment
   C. kidnapping
   D. luring
   E. aggravated sexual assault

The following fact pattern pertains to Questions 5–7.

Mercury Anderson, 50, took Candice Wesley, 29, from her automobile against her will. Anderson brought Wesley to a New Brunswick apartment and demanded a $50,000 ransom. For some reason, he released her at a diner six hours later, unharmed. Anderson was apprehended for the offense five months later but escaped from custody within a week.

5. Which of the following elements subjects Anderson to a kidnapping charge?

    A. He unlawfully removed Wesley from her car.
    B. He unlawfully confined Wesley in the New Brunswick apartment.
    C. He demanded a $50,000 ransom.
    D. all of the above
    E. none of the above

6. Which factor in Mercury Anderson's case is irrelevant under the kidnapping statute?

    A. Anderson's taking of Wesley from her car against her will
    B. Anderson's demanding a ransom
    C. Anderson's escaping after he was arrested
    D. the fact that Wesley was released unharmed
    E. all of the above

7. Mercury Anderson most appropriately should be charged with what?

    A. a second degree kidnapping because he released Wesley unharmed and in a safe place prior to apprehension
    B. a second degree kidnapping because the ransom demand did not exceed $100,000
    C. a second degree kidnapping because Wesley is an adult
    D. a first degree kidnapping because kidnapping is always a crime of the first degree
    E. a disorderly persons offense because his actions amounted to nothing more than harassment

The following fact pattern pertains to Questions 8 and 9.

Bethany Anderson had the sole physical and legal custody of Rainbow Anderson, age 10. Mercury Anderson, Rainbow's father, secretly took his daughter from Bethany. Mercury Anderson kept the minor in his custody for three years, never advising Bethany of her child's whereabouts.

Rainbow was never harmed by Anderson. The police captured Anderson, with Rainbow, in a hideaway house in Sussex County.

8. The best offense to charge Mercury Anderson with is:

   A. interference of custody, not kidnapping, because the abducted child was the daughter of Anderson

   B. interference of custody, not kidnapping, because the abducted child was not harmed by Anderson

   C. kidnapping, not interference of custody, because Anderson's actions amounted to permanently depriving the mother of her lawful custody of the child

   D. neither kidnapping nor interference of custody but criminal restraint since Anderson did not harm his daughter

   E. neither kidnapping nor interference of custody but false imprisonment since Anderson did not harm his daughter

9. What would be an affirmative defense for Mercury Anderson by which he could avoid any criminal conviction for his taking of Rainbow?

   A. if Anderson had a pending custody action in family court

   B. if Anderson had a psychological report from a licensed medical doctor, stating that Bethany Anderson was legally insane

   C. if Anderson was advised by a police officer or prosecutor that he could legally take Rainbow

   D. if Rainbow was 15 years old—not 10—when Mercury Anderson took her, and Anderson did not take her with the purpose to commit a crime against or with her

   E. There is no affirmative defense available to him.

10. Mercury Anderson, 50, enticed Frank Pileggi, 10, into a car by offering the boy a set of baseball cards. Once inside the automobile, Anderson committed the offense of aggravated criminal sexual contact by rubbing Pileggi's buttocks and groin area. He then released the boy. In addition to aggravated criminal sexual contact, with what other offense should Anderson be charged?

   A. criminal coercion
   B. harassment
   C. disorderly conduct
   D. luring
   E. post-partum depression

11. Virginia can't find her 13-year-old son, Marcus, who has wandered off in the Willowbrook Mall. Finally, she locates him, chastises him, and takes him to the car. Once in the car, Virginia won't let Marcus leave, although he is demanding to be let out to go back into the mall. After about 10 minutes of arguing, Virginia drives off, taking Marcus back home. With which of the following offenses should Virginia be charged?

   A. kidnapping
   B. criminal restraint
   C. false imprisonment
   D. interference with custody
   E. nothing, because she has an affirmative defense in that her sole purpose was to assume control of her minor child

14

Sexual Offenses

1. Aggravated sexual assault is:

    A. a first degree crime
    B. a second degree crime
    C. a third degree crime
    D. a fourth degree crime
    E. a disorderly persons offense

2. Martin kidnaps Kerry, 25, taking her to a cave in Sparta. There, against her will, Martin forces Kerry to have sexual intercourse with him. Kerry does not suffer severe personal injury and does not go to the hospital after the attack. Which is the most appropriate offense to charge Martin with?

   A. aggravated sexual assault because nonconsensual sexual intercourse occurred during a kidnapping
   B. aggravated sexual assault because nonconsensual sexual intercourse is always an act of aggravated sexual assault
   C. sexual assault because Kerry did not suffer severe personal injury
   D. sexual assault because Kerry did not go to the hospital
   E. none of the above because without a hospital report, it would be too difficult to prove anything

3. Assume some facts as above, except Martin does not kidnap Kerry. The nonconsensual intercourse occurs during a "date rape" at Kerry's apartment. What is the most appropriate offense to charge Martin with?

   A. aggravated sexual assault because nonconsensual sexual intercourse is always an act of aggravated sexual assault
   B. sexual assault because Kerry did not suffer severe personal injury and because no other necessary factor existed that would elevate the offense to aggravated sexual assault
   C. sexual assault because Kerry did not go to the hospital
   D. sexual assault because the act occurred during a "date rape"
   E. none of the above because without a hospital report, it would be too difficult to prove anything

4. In a Hoboken alley, Mercury Anderson exposed his genitals to 20-year-old Eric Mesos. Mesos, disgusted, reported the act to the Hoboken Police Department. In this action, Anderson could be convicted of what offense?

    A. reckless endangerment
    B. invasion of privacy
    C. luring
    D. involuntary servitude
    E. lewdness

5. Mercury Anderson hid in the office of 26-year-old attorney Kami Subron. There he consumed beer and secretly watched Subron engage in sexual intercourse with her lover, Suave. For his secret voyeurism, with what offense should Anderson be charged?

    A. luring
    B. scanning
    C. invasion of privacy
    D. lewdness
    E. all of the above

6. What is always an element of aggravated sexual assault?

    A. nonconsensual sexual intercourse
    B. nonconsensual sexual contact
    C. sexual penetration
    D. violence
    E. all of the above

7. Mercury Anderson met Samantha Cora, 12, at a carnival. He bought her cotton candy and ice cream and then asked if she would join him at his apartment. Cora agreed, and at the apartment, she consensually engaged in sexual intercourse with Anderson. Anderson is guilty of which offense?

    A. nothing, the act was consensual
    B. aggravated criminal sexual contact
    C. sexual assault
    D. aggravated sexual assault
    E. kidnapping

8. Janice, using physical force, grabs Melinda's breast through Melinda's clothing. Janice did this for her own sexual gratification. Melinda, an adult, did not consent to this touching. Janice is guilty of what offense?

   A. aggravated sexual assault
   B. sexual assault
   C. aggravated criminal sexual contact
   D. criminal sexual contact
   E. invasion of privacy

9. Assume the same facts as above, but Melinda is 12 and Janice is her math teacher. What offense is Janice guilty of violating?

   A. aggravated sexual assault
   B. sexual assault
   C. aggravated criminal sexual contact
   D. criminal sexual contact
   E. invasion of privacy

10. Under which circumstance is lewdness elevated from a disorderly persons offense to a fourth degree crime?

   A. Bill exposes his genitals to Mary, 40, in a public park.
   B. Karla exposes her breasts to Mike, 23, at a major league baseball game.
   C. Stephanie moons Frankie, 18, in a church parking lot.
   D. Davon exposes his genitals to Cheryl, 11, in a parking lot.
   E. all of the above

11. In a department store, Mercury Anderson set up a hidden camera in the women's dressing room. There, he videotaped Kami Subron, naked, as she changed into various articles of lingerie. What is the best offense with which to charge Anderson?

   A. a disorderly persons offense of invasion of privacy
   B. a third degree crime of invasion of privacy
   C. a fourth degree crime of peering
   D. a petty disorderly persons offense of disorderly conduct
   E. Unfortunately, Anderson's actions do not amount to an offense because people must expect that they may be videotaped in a dressing room.

12. Smitty holds a loaded pistol to Jamaal's head and then forces Jamaal to engage in anal intercourse with him. He then shoots and kills Jamaal. With what offense should Smitty be charged?

   A. murder
   B. sexual assault
   C. aggravated sexual assault
   D. a and b
   E. a and c

13. Chooch, a corrections officer at the Passaic County Jail, engages in consensual fellatio with Babs, an inmate at the jail. Chooch is guilty of what?

   A. aggravated sexual assault
   B. sexual assault
   C. aggravated criminal sexual contact
   D. criminal sexual contact
   E. no offense at all—the fellatio was consensual

14. What is *not* an act of sexual penetration?

    A. insertion of a finger in another's anus
    B. insertion of a finger in another's vagina
    C. insertion of a finger between another's breasts
    D. cunnilingus
    E. fellatio

15. Granny, 72, rubs the groin of Perry, her 15-yer-old grandson, without Perry's consent. Granny does this because she's attempting to wipe tomato sauce off Perry's pants. Granny is guilty of what offense?

    A. aggravated criminal sexual contact
    B. criminal sexual contact
    C. invasion of privacy
    D. luring
    E. no offense because she did not rub her grandson's groin to sexually gratify herself or to humiliate him

16. Aggravated criminal sexual contact is a:

    A. first degree crime
    B. third degree crime
    C. disorderly persons offense
    D. petty disorderly persons offense
    E. misdemeanor

17. Marshall Crumb videotapes Kim engaging in cunnilingus with Michelle in a public park. Can Marshall be convicted of invasion of privacy?

   A. no, because Kim and Michelle did not have a reasonable expectation that they would not be observed
   B. no, because cunnilingus is not an act of sexual penetration
   C. yes, because Kim and Michelle did not consent to the videotaping
   D. yes, because Kim and Michelle had obtained a marriage license in Massachusetts
   E. a and b only

18. Stewart has committed an act of invasion of privacy, secretly watching Laura, 30, take a shower. This act would be elevated from a fourth degree crime to a third degree crime if:

   A. Stewart was actually in the room, watching Laura take her shower
   B. Stewart photographed Laura while she was taking her shower
   C. Stewart told friends about his illicit watching of Laura in the shower
   D. Stewart played the banjo while watching Laura in the shower
   E. none of the above

19. Assume the same facts as above, but Stewart also masturbates while watching Laura in the shower. What is the best additional offense with which to charge Stewart?

   A. lewdness if he reasonably expected that Laura would see him masturbating
   B. luring if he tried to entice Laura
   C. criminal sexual contact under all circumstances
   D. peeping Tom because he was watching
   E. all of the above

20. Chumley has consensual sexual intercourse with his neighbor Carol, 32, who is mentally defective. Of what offense could Chumley be convicted?

    A. attempted murder because she was mentally defective and could have perished during the intercourse
    B. disorderly conduct because the act was probably tumultuous
    C. aggravated sexual assault if the state could prove that he knew or should have known that Carol was mentally defective
    D. aggravated sexual assault regardless of what he knew or should have known about Carol's mental abilities
    E. nothing, the sexual intercourse was consensual

21. Joan rubs Esmeralda's vagina as she is taking a bath. Esmeralda is 17 and the act was consented to. Joan can be convicted of what offense?

    A. criminal sexual contact if Esmeralda is related to Joan by blood as a first cousin
    B. criminal sexual contact if Joan is Esmeralda's volleyball coach
    C. criminal sexual contact if Joan is Eseralda's foster parent
    D. nothing, if Joan knew Esmeralda only from the restaurant where she works as a waitress
    E. all of the above

22. Criminal sexual contact is:

    A. a second degree crime
    B. a fourth degree crime
    C. a disorderly persons offense
    D. a petty disorderly persons offense
    E. a misdemeanor

15

Robbery

1. Robbery of an automobile is considered carjacking if during the unlawful taking:

   A. the actor inflicts bodily injury upon an occupant of the vehicle
   B. the actor threatens an occupant of the vehicle with immediate bodily injury
   C. the actor threatens an occupant of the vehicle with arson
   D. all of the above
   E. none of the above

2. Tubby grabs Sissy by the arm in a Cherry Hill bar. He threatens to rape her if she does not turn over $1,000 in cash to him. Sissy gives Tubby the money and then leaves. What is the *best* offense for Cherry Hill Police to charge Tubby with?

   A. attempted aggravated sexual assault
   B. attempted kidnapping
   C. attempted murder
   D. first degree robbery
   E. second degree robbery

The following fact pattern pertains to Questions 3 and 4.

Mickey Vice enters Nelson Simone's BMW and violently pistol whips him, leaving him unconscious in the passenger seat. Vice kisses Simone on the lips and then speeds off in the vehicle, driving from Paramus to New Brunswick. Once in New Brunswick, Vice exits the vehicle and proceeds to a gas station where he breaks the attendant's nose while stealing a gas canister and cigarettes from him.

3. For his actions leveled against Simone, what is the best offense to charge Mickey Vice with?

   A. carjacking
   B. aggravated assault
   C. aggravated sexual assault
   D. all of the above
   E. a and b only

4. What offense is Vice guilty of for his unlawful taking of the gas canister and cigarettes?

   A. second degree robbery because breaking the attendant's nose amounts to only *bodily injury,* not *serious bodily injury*
   B. first degree robbery if he was armed with a pistol during the offense
   C. carjacking because the offense occurred at a gas station
   D. a and b only
   E. a and c only

5. Robbery is distinct from theft:

   A. because robbery involves the use of weapons
   B. because robbery involves inflicting bodily injury
   C. because robbery can be a crime of the first degree and theft cannot
   D. all of the above
   E. none of the above

6. While Snake is in the outhouse, Goose jumps into the driver seat of Snake's pickup truck and begins to drive off. Snake, alerted to Goose's driving by the rumbling of the truck's muffler, hurriedly exits the outhouse and chases Goose down, catching him at a red light. Snake rips Goose from the truck and physically beats him. Snake then drives off, leaving Goose with two less teeth and a concussion. Snake is guilty of what offense?

   A. carjacking because Snake inflicted bodily injury upon Goose in taking the truck back
   B. robbery, not carjacking, because the vehicle belonged to Goose
   C. neither carjacking nor robbery because there was no unlawful taking by Snake
   D. neither carjacking nor robbery because the truck obviously was of little value
   E. none of the above

7. Carjacking is a:

   A. first degree crime
   B. second degree crime
   C. first or second degree crime
   D. third or fourth degree crime
   E. all of the above

16

Bias Crimes

1. Which of the following offenses *cannot* trigger a bias intimidation charge even if the offense was carried out with a purpose to intimidate a person in one of the protected groups enumerated under the statute?

   A. murder
   B. kidnapping
   C. criminal restraint
   D. burglary
   E. theft

2. Allan loses a chess game to Junior, a Catholic man. After the chess game, Allan stabs Junior in the chest. Junior survives the attack. What offense is Allan guilty of violating?

   A. aggravated assault because of the deadly weapon involved
   B. simple assault because he survived
   C. bias intimidation if the stabbing was committed with a purpose to intimidate the victim because of his Catholic religion
   D. a and c only
   E. b and c only

The following fact pattern pertains to Questions 3 and 4.

Charlotte is a resident of Maplewood. She has short blond hair and is a Mormon. She was born in Cuba and once broke her nose in a boxing match. Charlotte also previously posed naked in a magazine and is heterosexual. Her hobbies include baking, flying kites, and plumbing. Pat sexually assaulted Charlotte with a purpose to intimidate her because of something in her personal background.

3. What part of Charlotte's background could *not* trigger a bias intimidation charge?

   A. her Cuban ethnicity
   B. that she is heterosexual
   C. that she resides in Maplewood
   D. a and b only
   E. b and c only

4. What part of Charlotte's background could trigger a bias intimidation charge against Pat?

   A. her blond hair
   B. her past broken nose
   C. her plumbing hobby
   D. all of the above
   E. none of the above

5. If Pat sexually assaulted Charlotte based solely upon the fact that Charlotte is a woman, could he be convicted of bias intimidation?

   A. no, because of the gender exemptions in sexual offenses
   B. no, because she has blond hair
   C. yes, because gender is a protected class
   D. yes, because women have special protections under the statute
   E. yes, because of *res ipsa loquitor*

6. Bias intimidation is a:

    A. fourth degree crime if the underlying offense is a disorderly persons offense

    B. fourth degree crime if the underlying offense is a petty disorderly persons offense

    C. first degree crime if the underlying offense is a second degree crime

    D. first degree crime if the underlying offense is a first degree crime

    E. all of the above

Arson, Criminal Mischief, and Other Property Destruction

The following fact pattern pertains to Questions 1 and 2.

After munching on a raw potato, Maglio smashed the remainder of it into the car window of Carlos, his nemesis. The window broke, resulting in $205.00 damage to Carlos's car.

1. The best offense to charge Maglio with for damaging Carlos's car is what?

   A. defiant trespass
   B. burglary
   C. criminal mischief
   D. peering into windows
   E. vegetative destruction

2. The degree of Maglio's offense is which of these?

   A. disorderly persons offense because the pecuniary loss was $500 or less
   B. fourth degree crime because the pecuniary loss was more than $200 but less than $500
   C. disorderly persons offense because the property damaged was a private automobile, not a private plane
   D. petty disorderly persons offense because of the *rex tex tung* doctrine
   E. a and c only

3. Mickey Vice removed the vehicle identification number from a 1977 Chevy Impala that he stole in Camden. For removing the VIN, what is the best offense for Camden Police to charge Vice with?

   A. carjacking under 2C:15-2
   B. theft under 2C:20-3
   C. burglary under 2C:18-2
   D. criminal mischief under 2C:17-3
   E. removal of motor vehicle identification number under 2C:17-6

4. Mickey Vice shot at nuclear power plant employees and threw a stick of dynamite into nuclear-generating machinery, hoping to cause radiation, but no radiation was actually released. Mickey Vice is guilty of which of the following?

   A. a third degree crime because although he tried to damage the nuclear plant, no radiation was actually released
   B. a first degree crime because his purpose in throwing dynamite into the nuclear machinery was to release radiation
   C. a disorderly persons offense because the damage was obviously nil
   D. all of the above
   E. none of the above

5. Mickey Vice placed and detonated dynamite at the base of the building of his father-in-law, located in Paterson. Over 30 homes were destroyed, and numerous people suffered serious bodily injuries. Mickey Vice is guilty of what offense?

   A. arson
   B. aggravated arson
   C. aggravated assault
   D. a and c
   E. b and c

6. Criminal mischief is:

   A. a crime of the third degree
   B. a crime of the fourth degree
   C. a disorderly persons offense
   D. all of the above
   E. none of the above

7. Maria always hated her brother Bobby's baseball card collection. Although now they are adults, both still hang out in their tree house located in their parents' backyard. One day, Maria stopped by Mommy and Daddy's house and went directly to the tree house. There, at the base of the tree, was Bobby's baseball card collection. In a sudden fit of rage, Maria poured gasoline on the cards, lit them, and ran away. The result was the burning and complete destruction of the baseball cards and the tree house. Bobby, unbeknownst to Maria, was in the tree house at the time of the fire, but he escaped without injury. Which of the following is the best offense to charge Maria with?

   A. aggravated arson
   B. arson
   C. criminal mischief
   D. reckless endangerment
   E. disorderly conduct

8. Assume the same facts as above, but Maria takes the baseball cards from the tree house to the fireplace inside the house. There, she burns them and then safely puts out the fire. With what offense should Maria be charged?

    A. aggravated arson
    B. arson
    C. criminal mischief
    D. reckless endangerment
    E. no offense at all because the fire was safely put out

9. Jordi flew in from Chicago to visit Veronica at her new three-bedroom ranch in Wyckoff. While Veronica was at work, Jordi put a log in the fireplace and ignited it with the aid of a newspaper. The fire accidentally grew out of control, though, catching nearby drapes. Jordi, nervous and embarrassed, ran out of the house, which was now engulfed in flames. She drove to Garden State Mall to pass some time, and then came back to the ranch and watched the volunteer firefighters put out the blaze. Veronica's new ranch was completely destroyed. Wyckoff Police should charge Jordi with what offense?

    A. nothing, the fire started accidentally
    B. a fourth degree crime for failing to report a dangerous fire
    C. a third degree crime of arson
    D. a disorderly persons offense of arson
    E. aggravated arson because the structure was completely destroyed by the fire

10. Assume the same facts as above, except Jordi purposely burned down Veronica's house because she was jealous of her. Here, Jordi is guilty of what offense?

    A. aggravated arson
    B. arson
    C. manslaughter
    D. a and c
    E. b and c

The following fact pattern pertains to Questions 11 and 12.

Eli goes to the newly created dam in Passaic and purposely causes an explosion with the intent to cause a flood. The dam indeed breaks and water floods half of the city of Passaic, resulting in millions of dollars in property damage, including the destruction of more than 100 families' homes.

11. Eli is guilty of:

    A. a second degree crime for causing widespread damage
    B. a fourth degree crime for causing widespread damage
    C. arson
    D. a and c
    E. b and c

12. Instead of the dam breaking, Eli accidentally blows his arm off. No damage at all occurs to the City of Passaic or the dam. Eli should be charged with which of the following offenses?

    A. a second degree crime for attempting to cause widespread damage
    B. a fourth degree crime for attempting to cause widespread damage
    C. criminal mischief because no damage actually occurred to the dam or the City of Passaic
    D. attempted manslaughter of himself
    E. stupido idiosis

13. An act of arson, a crime of the third degree, has occurred if:

    A. Theresa starts a fire at Kelly's house with the
       purpose of killing her
    B. Theresa starts a fire at Kelly's house with the
       purpose of destroying the house
    C. Theresa starts a fire in her own house under
       circumstances that put her mother in danger of
       death, with the purpose of collecting insurance
       on the destroyed house
    D. all of the above
    E. none of the above

14. Jack and Mack go to Sterling Forest with a case of beer and a
    pound of hash. Once they reach a particularly secluded, wooded
    area, they lay the hash out on the ground and light it up. Their
    purpose is to absorb as much hash smoke as possible, seeking "a
    new kind of high." Unfortunately, the burning hash ignites some
    nearby fallen leaves. The two men run off, laughing. The fire ulti-
    mately burns down a couple hundred trees. Jack and Mack should
    be charged with what offense for the fire they started?

    A. trespassing
    B. criminal mischief
    C. arson
    D. aggravated arson
    E. rubbish burning

15. Aggravated arson becomes a crime of the first degree under
    which of the following circumstances?

    A. Leroy purposely burns down his house, aware
       that the blaze could kill his sleeping wife.
    B. Leroy pays Julio $1,000 to burn down his house,
       aware that the blaze could kill his sleeping wife.
    C. Leroy purposely starts an electrical fire in his
       friend's house, with the purpose of destroying it.
    D. all of the above
    E. a and b only

16. Josh purposely breaks a bulb in a stop light in Somerville. He is guilty of:

    A. a crime of the first degree
    B. a crime of the third degree
    C. a disorderly persons offense
    D. an infraction
    E. a contraction

17. Instead of purposely breaking the stop light bulb, Josh, "for kicks," climbs up the light and swings on it, accidentally causing the bulb to break. Here, Josh is guilty of:

    A. a crime of the first degree
    B. a crime of the third degree
    C. a disorderly persons offense
    D. nothing, the damage was an accident
    E. a contracting infraction

18. Mickey Vice explodes dynamite in nuclear power plant machinery with the purpose of releasing radiation. Five hundred people are killed, thousands of others seriously injured, and 50 miles of property are severely damaged by the radiation leak. In addition to murder, Vice is guilty of:

    A. a second degree crime of aggravated arson
    B. a second degree crime of causing widespread injury and damage
    C. a first degree crime of purposely damaging nuclear power plant machinery that results in death
    D. all of the above
    E. a and b only

19. Stupid Sam purposely defaces a heliport in Newark, making the landing area uneven and slippery. When the next helicopter arrived, it tumbled over due to Stupid Sam's mischievous activities. The pilot was killed as a result. In addition to a homicide offense, with what else could Stupid Sam be charged?

   A. aggravated arson
   B. arson
   C. a disorderly persons offense of criminal mischief
   D. a second degree crime of criminal mischief
   E. There's nothing in the code to additionally charge him with.

Burglary and Other Criminal Intrusion

1. Ignacio Marini used a screwdriver to pry open a screen and illegally enter a home in Mahwah. His purpose of entering the house was to steal a gerbil inside it. What is the *best* offense with which to charge Marini?

   A. defiant trespass
   B. burglary
   C. peering into windows
   D. robbery
   E. harassment

2. The primary difference between theft and burglary is:

   A. a theft involves the taking of money
   B. burglary involves wearing a mask
   C. burglary involves entering a structure with the intent to commit an offense once inside
   D. burglary requires surreptitiously gaining access to a dwelling with burglary tools
   E. theft is a crime of the second degree

3. A horse farm is clearly marked with "No Trespassing" signs. Bigby sees the signs, ignores them, and enters the farm. Once there, he consumes two cans of cola and a beer. Bigby is guilty of:

   A. defiant trespass
   B. burglary
   C. drinking in public
   D. cola-ascoptemy
   E. partying

4. Burglary becomes a crime of the second degree when:

   A. the defendant inflicts bodily injury upon a
      victim
   B. the defendant threatens bodily injury upon a
      victim
   C. the defendant is armed with a deadly weapon
   D. all of the above
   E. a and c only

5. Alex converses with Ellen on the phone. During their conversation, Ellen tells Alex to come by her house and look into her kitchen window because she "has a surprise for him." Alex follows her instructions, stops by, looks in her window, and sees Ellen, completely naked, baking cookies. Alex is guilty of what offense?

   A. burglary
   B. defiant trespass
   C. fourth degree peering into windows
   D. disorderly persons offense of peering into
      windows
   E. no offense at all

6. Which of the following actions constitutes a burglary?

   A. Peter is told by Paul not to step foot on his lawn. Peter ignores Paul, runs onto Paul's lawn, and square-dances with Paul's wife on the greenery.

   B. Mambo pickpockets Eric in the county park, stealing $100 cash and a carrot.

   C. Gooney climbs a tree with the intent to watch Caroline undress in her bedroom. Gooney succeeds.

   D. Fidel cuts a hole through the roof of Sharon's house in order to sexually assault her. Fidel carries out his plan and rapes Sharon in her bedroom.

   E. Sharman squeezes Scott in the den.

Theft and Related Offenses

1. Chacon and Maple are adult brothers who live in the same house. Chacon steals $1,000 cash off Maple's dresser. Chacon is guilty of:

   A. second degree theft
   B. third degree theft
   C. second degree burglary
   D. a and c
   E. b and c

2. The following is an example of a second degree theft:

   A. Gary steals 2 kilograms of cocaine from Jason.
   B. Maude heists the human remains of her former boss from a funeral parlor.
   C. Penelope, knowing she has only $200 to her name, has Robert build a shore house for her at a cost of $450,000. Penelope never pays Bob.
   D. all of the above
   E. none of the above

3. Mickey Morabito maintained and operated a shop in East Rutherford where he routinely bought stolen automobiles from various thieves. He either immediately resold the vehicles for a huge profit or chopped them up and then sold the stolen parts. Morabito could be convicted of which offense?

   A. theft by extortion
   B. fencing
   C. being the leader of auto trafficking network
   D. all of the above
   E. b and c only

The following fact pattern pertains to Questions 4 and 5.

Ignacio Marini stole a box of Devil Dogs worth $9.95 from a supermarket in Maywood. Afterward, he went to a department store in Paramus, picked out a gold watch valued at $22,000, and left without paying for it.

4. For the Devil Dogs theft, the best offense to charge Marini with is:

   A. theft by deception
   B. theft of services
   C. shoplifting
   D. receiving stolen property
   E. all of the above

5. For his theft of the $22,000 gold watch, Marini should be charged with:

   A. fencing
   B. being the leader of a shoplifting network
   C. third degree shoplifting
   D. fourth degree shoplifting
   E. a disorderly persons offense of shoplifting because shoplifting is always a disorderly persons offense

The following fact pattern pertains to Questions 6 and 7.

Mark is in the pawnbroker business. He regularly buys items of jewelry, television sets, stereos, and home appliances. Jerry, a man who Mark knows to be a drug addict, stops by his store with a diamond ring. Mark asks Jerry neither for proof of ownership of the ring (i.e., a receipt or warranty) nor where he obtained the ring. The ring, valued at $110,000, turns out to have been stolen by Jerry.

6. Mark could be convicted of what offense?

    A. theft by extortion because he could have exposed Jerry as a drug addict
    B. theft by deception because he reinforced a false impression that the ring was lawfully obtained
    C. shoplifting because the ring is a stolen good now for sale in a lawful business
    D. receiving stolen property because, under the circumstances, he is presumed to have knowledge that the ring was stolen
    E. theft of services because he knowingly converted the ring to his benefit

7. For stealing the ring, Jerry is guilty of:

    A. first degree theft
    B. second degree theft
    C. third degree theft
    D. an additional count of grand larceny
    E. *modus operendi*

8. Ignacio Marini stole a television set and defaced the serial numbers on the set. Franz Bellenwood, who owns an electronics store, told Marini to bring the TV set to Bellenwood's basement, where numerous stolen appliances with defaced serial numbers were stored. It was Bellenwood's plan to sell the stolen TV along with the other items in the basement. Bellenwood traded a half-carat diamond earring for the TV. Bellenwood should be charged with what offense?

    A. fencing
    B. being the leader of a shoplifting network
    C. theft of property delivered by mistake
    D. concealment
    E. all of the above

9. A person who knowingly rides as a passenger in a motor vehicle that is being operated without the owner's consent is guilty of:

    A. a first degree crime
    B. a fourth degree crime
    C. a petty disorderly persons offense
    D. a motor vehicle offense under 39:3-40
    E. no offense at all because he was just a passenger and isn't culpable for the driver's heist of the vehicle

10. A $25,000 insurance check was delivered to Ignacio Marini by mistake. The true recipient of the check was Marini's uncle—and Marini knew this. With the purpose to deprive his uncle of the proceeds of the check, Marini deposited the $25,000 into his personal bank account. What is the most appropriate offense with which to charge Marini?

    A. receiving stolen property under 2C:20-7
    B. fencing under 2C:20-7.1
    C. theft by extortion under 2C:20-5
    D. theft of property delivered by mistake under 2C:20-6
    E. nothing, it is a civil action

11. Perry, a millionaire, is invited into Mortisha's house to snack on some apple pie. Once inside, Perry slithers into Mortisha's bedroom and takes food stamp coupons, valued at $1,000, from her dresser. The next day, Perry binges on $1,000 worth of potato chips, cakes, cookies, kobe beef, and coconuts that he bought with Mortisha's food stamps. Perry's use of Mortisha's food stamps is:

    A. a misdemeanor
    B. a petty disorderly persons offense
    C. a fourth degree crime
    D. a federal offense only
    E. stupid, because he's going to make himself fat

12. Ignacio Marini and an owner of a horse farm shook hands on a deal that required Marini to make four payments of $1,000 in exchange for a prize moose. Marini took the moose but never made the payments. Which of the following statements is true?

    A. Marini could be convicted of an offense under 2C:20-9 for theft by failure to make required disposition if he purposely obtained the moose with no intention of ever making the payments.
    B. If Marini is guilty of a theft under 2C:20-9, it would be a third degree crime because the value involved exceeds $500 but is less than $75,000.
    C. Marini could not be convicted of any offense in the criminal code because this is purely a contract dispute.
    D. a and b only
    E. none of the above

13. Which of the following circumstances would render Sol guilty of theft by extortion?

    A. Sol threatens to inflict bodily injury upon Julie if Julie doesn't sign over the title of her car to him.

    B. Sol tells Sandy that if she doesn't turn over her diamond pinky ring to him, he will tell the media that she regularly frequents a nudist camp.

    C. Jim is a defendant in a civil suit. Sol threatens to testify against Jim if Jim does not give Sol the motorcycle in his garage.

    D. all of the above

    E. a and b only

14. Theft by extortion:

    A. can be a crime of the first, second, third, or fourth degree, depending upon the monetary value involved in the act

    B. is always a crime of the second degree, regardless of the monetary value involved

    C. must be a purposeful act

    D. a and c

    E. b and c

The following fact pattern pertains to Questions 15 and 16.

Posing as the Paramus tax collector, Ignacio Marini advised 73-year-old Alzheimer's sufferer Fanny Moses that she was $52,500 in arrears in her property taxes. Moses, believing Marini, turned over a $52,500 check to Marini. The truth is that Moses was not in arrears at all and Marini was not the Paramus tax collector.

15. Marini's actions are a classic example of what offense?

    A. theft of property mislaid under 2C:20-6

    B. theft by deception under 2C:20-4

    C. theft by failure to make required disposition under 2C:20-9

    D. receiving stolen property under 2C:20-7

    E. This is not an offense at all because Moses voluntarily wrote the check to Marini.

16. Marini's taking of Fanny Moses' $52,500 check is:

    A. a first degree crime

    B. a second degree crime

    C. a third degree crime

    D. a petty disorderly persons offense

    E. not an offense at all because Moses voluntarily wrote the check to Marini

21

Forgery and Fraudulent Practices

1. Maxwell Borscht created a sham Ernest Hemingway manuscript with the purpose to defraud Holly. Borscht traded the fake manuscript to Holly for a washer/dryer set. Which of the following is the *best* offense to charge Borscht with?

   A. offering a false instrument for filing under 2C:21-3
   B. criminal simulation under 2C:21-2
   C. criminal solicitation under 2C:21-38
   D. piracy under common law
   E. all of the above

2. Which of the following acts violates the New Jersey Trademark Counterfeiting Act under 2C:21-32?

   A. Artie manufactures 1,000 chimney sweepers, branding each sweeper with the label "Fresco Chimney Sweepers," knowing that the famous sweeper company was not involved with Artie's sweepers.

   B. Mitchell advertises the sale of "Gucci wallets," knowing that the wallets were rip-offs of the Gucci company.

   C. GeorgeAnne possesses five fake Tag Heuer watches. She wears them frequently, showing them off.

   D. all of the above

   E. a and b only

3. Adams lends Washington $25,000 at an interest rate of 27% per annum. Adams is guilty of what?

   A. first degree usury

   B. third degree usury

   C. a disorderly persons offense of usury

   D. loansharking

   E. no crime at all because lending money at 27% is legal

4. The Hunk fraudulently manufactures birth certificates in multiple persons' names. He commits these acts without those persons' authorization and then sells the birth certificates to eager buyers. The Hunk is guilty of what?

   A. a fourth degree crime if only three different birth certificates were manufactured
   B. a third degree crime if he manufactured seven birth certificates under seven separate individuals' names
   C. a second degree crime if he manufactured 25 birth certificates under separate individuals' names
   D. all of the above
   E. The Hunk's activities would always be a second degree crime.

5. Maxwell Borscht submits inaccurate financial statements as to the fiscal condition of his company to Sundry Bank in order to obtain a loan. Here Borscht is guilty of:

   A. a third degree crime if he issued the financial statements knowing that they were false and in an effort to deceive the bank
   B. a first degree crime if Borscht was the CEO or president of his company
   C. no crime at all if he did not know the financial statements were inaccurate
   D. a and c only
   E. b and c only

The following fact pattern pertains to Questions 6 and 7.

Michael "The Hunk" Pardemena "restructured" Salvatore Rando's will making Salvatore's son, Manny, the sole beneficiary. The Hunk did this by dissolving the printed ink and replacing it with language favorable to Rando.

6. The *best* offense to charge The Hunk with is what?

   A. criminal simulation
   B. forgery
   C. fraud related to public records
   D. falsifying financial statements
   E. a disorderly persons offense

7. The degree of The Hunk's offense is what?

   A. a first degree crime
   B. a third degree crime
   C. a disorderly persons offense
   D. a misdemeanor
   E. none of the above

8. Manny Rando, a truck driver, sold a currently valid Elizabeth Police badge to Michael, a cab driver. Which of the following statements is true?

   A. Rando, the seller, is guilty of a disorderly persons offense.
   B. Michael, the buyer, is guilty of a disorderly persons offense.
   C. Rando, the seller, is guilty of a third degree crime.
   D. a and b
   E. b and c

9. Assume the same facts as above, except Rando is an Elizabeth Police officer and he lends his badge to Michael. Here, Rando is guilty of:

   A. a disorderly persons offense
   B. a third degree crime
   C. no offense at all, but he could be fired
   D. no offense at all and he could be fired only if the badge wasn't polished
   E. no offense at all and he can't be fired

10. Maxwell Borscht, owner of a pizza parlor, had become insolvent and received the appropriate government notice that proceedings had been started for the repossession of the pizza parlor and all the materials he used in the business. The proceedings were initiated to repay creditors to which he owed money. Borscht decides he is not going to allow authorities to take his things and hides the various items in a warehouse that he secretly rented under another name. Here, Borscht is guilty of:

    A. a second degree crime of fraud in insolvency if the value of the items exceeded $75,000
    B. a third degree crime of fraud in insolvency if the value of the items exceeded $1,000 but was less than $75,000
    C. a fourth degree crime of fraud in insolvency if the value of the items was $1,000 or less
    D. all of the above
    E. There is no crime of fraud in insolvency. This is a civil action only.

11. Over time, Mabel has slipped dozens of slugs into her local laundromat's washing machines. The slugs, perfectly mimicking quarters, got her free cleaning to the tune of $1,500. Other than a theft charge, Mabel is guilty of what?

    A. a disorderly persons offense under 2C:21-18, the slug statute
    B. a third degree crime under 2C:21-18, the slug statute
    C. a first degree crime under 2C:21-22.4, the laundromat fraud statute
    D. all of the above
    E. none of the above

12. A person can be convicted of forgery:

    A. if, with reckless disregard of the truth, he alters a writing of another
    B. if, with reckless disregard of the truth, he lies on the witness stand
    C. if, with purpose to defraud another, he alters a writing of that person without that person's authorization
    D. if, with purpose to defraud the court, he lies on the witness stand
    E. all of the above

The following fact pattern pertains to Questions 13 and 14.

Jack "The Attack" Madison is scheduled to fight Will "The Thrill" Zambino in an upcoming heavyweight boxing match. Each boxer will receive a purse of $500,000. Slick Rick pays Will "The Thrill" $150,000 to go down in the fourth round, wherein Jack "The Attack" will be the victor. Will "The Thrill's" manager, Oscar, knows about the deal but fails to report it to authorities.

13. Slick Rick is guilty of what?

    A. a first degree crime because he initiated the rigging of the contest
    B. a second degree crime because the benefit conferred exceeded $75,000
    C. a fourth degree crime because the matter involved a sporting event but did not involve a public official
    D. a petty disorderly persons offense because both boxers were receiving payment ($500,000) for being in the fight
    E. no offense at all because boxing is a "self-regulated" sporting activity and the parties will be punished administratively

14. For not reporting the rigging of Will "The Thrill's" match, Will's manager, Oscar, is guilty of:

    A. a first degree crime
    B. a second degree crime
    C. a misdemeanor
    D. a disorderly persons offense
    E. no offense at all because boxing is a "self-regulated" sporting activity and the parties will be punished administratively

The following fact pattern pertains to Questions 15 and 16.

Maxwell Borscht earned $3,000,000 selling heroin. In an effort to disguise his illicit heroin sales, Borscht acted as if the $3,000,000 was earned through several pizza parlors he owned. He tallied receipts of pizzas, calzones, and strombolis in this multimillion dollar amount, deposited the funds into his business bank account and turned the records over to his accountant for reporting.

15. Based on this information, what offense is Borscht guilty of?

    A. insurance fraud
    B. credit card fraud
    C. money laundering
    D. usury
    E. c and d

16. Borscht's offense is:

    A. a crime of the first degree
    B. a crime of the third degree
    C. a crime of the fourth degree
    D. a petty disorderly persons offense
    E. a capital offense

17. Bart, a fireman, overhears Karla, a go-go dancer, explaining that she was arrested in Marlboro for a DWI. In an effort to impress Karla, Bert tells her that he is a lawyer and offers to represent her on the DWI in exchange for a few lap dances. Ultimately, Bart represents her in court, and Karla is convicted of the offense. Bart is guilty of what?

   A. a petty disorderly persons offense for the unauthorized practice of law
   B. a fourth degree crime for the unauthorized practice of law
   C. a first degree crime for the unauthorized practice of law
   D. a mandamus writ
   E. a bad rap

18. Which of the following acts does *not* constitute an act of usury?

   A. Premium Loan lends $5,000 to Bob, an individual, at an interest rate of 75% per annum.
   B. Premium Loan lends $500,000 to Smack Hack's Bar and Restaurant, a limited liability company, at an interest rate of 75% per annum.
   C. Marty lends $10,000 to his friend Jose, an individual, at an interest rate of 35% per annum.
   D. Marty lends $40,000 to Greg's Garbage Company, a corporation, at an interest rate of 57% per annum.
   E. Premium Loan lends $30,000 to Sunshine Shoe Service, a corporation, at 45% per annum.

19. A person who knowingly engages in the business of criminal usury is guilty of:

   A. a second degree crime
   B. a fourth degree crime
   C. a petty disorderly persons offense
   D. a bad business decision
   E. none of the above

The following fact pattern pertains to Questions 20 and 21.

Jameson issues a check in the amount of $15,000 to Schmidt in exchange for a pile of rare Idaho potatoes. The check bounces. Jameson eats the potatoes and never makes good on the check.

20. Which of the following statements is true?

    A. Jameson is guilty of issuing a "bad check" under 2C:21-5 if he knew that there were insufficient funds in his account at the time he issued the check.

    B. Jameson is guilty of issuing a "bad check" under 2C:21-5 if he knew that the bank account on which the check was written was closed when he issued the check.

    C. Jameson is not guilty of issuing a "bad check" under 2C:21-5 if Schmidt filed a timely civil action against him.

    D. all of the above

    E. a and b only

21. Jameson could *not* be convicted of issuing a "bad check" under 2C:21-5 if:

    A. he gave back at least half of the potatoes

    B. he was hospitalized because the potatoes were sour

    C. after receiving notice that there were insufficient funds in his bank account, he made good on the $15,000 check to Schmidt within 10 days

    D. a and c

    E. b and c

22

Disturbing Human Remains

1. A person commits a second degree crime if he:

   A. unearths a grave in a cemetery, pulling human remains from a casket and taking the clothes from the remains
   B. fails to dispose of human remains as required by law
   C. has sexual intercourse with human remains
   D. a and b
   E. a and c

Offenses Against the Family, Children, and Incompetents

1. State Senator Wilfredo Chavez attended a party where, all of a sudden, a guest popped a child pornography tape into the VCR. Which of the following statements is true?

   A. Senator Chavez is guilty of a fourth degree crime if he stayed at the party and watched the tape.
   B. Senator Chavez would be guilty of a second degree crime if he took the child porn tape and sold it to a friend.
   C. Senator Chavez is guilty of no offense if he did not watch the tape and left the party, disgusted.
   D. all of the above
   E. none of the above

The following fact pattern pertains to Questions 2 and 3.

Frank Roberts, 45, employed a 15-year-old boy to steal a camera. The camera was valued at $1,000.

2. For employing the 15-year-old boy to steal the camera, Roberts is guilty of:

   A. a third degree crime because the underlying theft offense is a third degree crime
   B. a second degree crime because the underlying theft offense is a second degree crime
   C. a second degree crime because the underlying theft offense is a third degree crime
   D. a disorderly persons offense because employing a minor to commit a criminal act is always a disorderly persons offense regardless of the underlying offense
   E. a common law breach of peace

3. If Roberts mistakenly but reasonably believed that the boy was 18 years of age or older, he:

   A. has an absolute affirmative defense
   B. has an affirmative defense if he also saw documentary identification of age, such as a driver's license, that a reasonable person would believe was valid
   C. has a presumption against guilt that would give rise to an affirmative defense
   D. is still guilty of a crime regardless of his mistaken, reasonable belief
   E. all of the above, depending upon modus operendi

4. Which of the following constitutes the third degree crime of abandoning/neglecting an elderly person or disabled adult?

   A. Barbie Penn is paid by her late father's estate to care for her 75-year-old mother on a daily basis. She locks her mother in her bedroom for 72 consecutive hours. The woman's only recourse for nutrition was tap water from the room's adjoining bathroom and two candy bars she had stashed in her bureau.

   B. Storm, 33, has a 54-year-old friend, Garth, who is paralyzed from the waist down. Storm frequently visits Garth, often bringing Garth to the supermarket to buy groceries. Storm, however, becomes angry at Garth when he caught his friend using his toothbrush. Storm decides not to visit Garth anymore. Ten weeks later, Garth is rushed to the hospital for lack of nutrition. His cupboards and refrigerator were barren.

   C. Sally Mae, 80, showed her daughter Ariel her will, which left everything to her. Ariel, a crack addict, nonetheless rarely visited Sally Mae, who was suffering from several ailments. Sally Mae, upset, told Ariel that she felt "abandoned," and threatened to remove her from the will. The next day, Sally Mae died of a heart attack.

   D. all of the above

   E. none of the above

5. Endangering the welfare of an incompetent person is:

   A. a first degree crime

   B. a third degree crime

   C. a disorderly persons offense

   D. a violation

   E. There is no such offense.

The following fact pattern pertains to Questions 6–9.

Cameraman Willie Maxso videotaped 10-year-old Suzie having sex with a 13-year-old boy. Suzie's mother, Barbie Penn, brought Suzie to Frank Roberts's house in order for the videotaping to occur. She watched the entire shoot. Roberts set up the shoot and thereafter made multiple copies of the videotape and sold them through the Internet.

6. For acting as the cameraman, Maxso is guilty of:

   A. a first degree crime if he knew the children's age
   B. a second degree crime as long as he wasn't the parent or guardian of one of the children
   C. a fourth degree crime if his only role was to film the children
   D. all of the above
   E. a and b only

7. If the children weren't actually having sexual intercourse, but were "simulating" sex, Maxso would be guilty of:

   A. no offense at all because the act was not real
   B. a disorderly persons offense because the "simulation" lowers the degree
   C. a fourth degree crime if his only role was to film the children
   D. a second degree crime as long as he wasn't the parent or guardian of one of the children
   E. a capital offense

8. Barbie Penn, Suzie's mother, is guilty of:

   A. a first degree crime
   B. a second degree crime
   C. a fourth degree crime
   D. a petty disorderly persons offense
   E. *res ipsa loquitor*

9. For selling the videotape of the two children's sexual acts, Frank Roberts is guilty of:

   A. a first degree crime
   B. a second degree crime
   C. a fourth degree crime
   D. a petty disorderly persons offense
   E. *res ipsa loquitor*

The following fact pattern pertains to Questions 10 and 11.

Barbie Penn purposely engaged in sexual intercourse—with two men at once—in front of her 10-year-old daughter, Suzie.

10. The two men are guilty of endangering the welfare of a child because:

    A. Suzie is under 16
    B. their sexual conduct would impair or debauch the morals of Suzie
    C. the doctrine of merger applies
    D. the men are not guilty of a child endangerment offense because they did not have a legal duty of care for Suzie and did not physically involve her in the sexual activity
    E. a and b

11. Barbie Penn is guilty of what offense for having sexual intercourse with the two men in front of her daughter?

    A. a disorderly persons offense of endangering the welfare of a child because she did not physically involve her daughter in the sexual act
    B. a third degree crime of endangering the welfare of a child because there was more than one sexual partner involved with her
    C. a second degree crime of endangering the welfare of a child because as Suzie's mother, she had a legal duty to care for her
    D. the offense of merger
    E. none of the above

25

Domestic Violence

1. Patrolman Terry Simon of the Kenilworth Police Department responds to a call of an argument at the McMoose home. Upon arriving, Officer Simon finds Mr. McMoose and Mrs. McMoose yelling at each other on the front porch of the home. Mr. McMoose, a champion powerlifter and nearly 300 pounds in weight, is bleeding from the nose. Mrs. McMoose is slight, weighing 100 pounds, and has no visible signs of injuries. Both Mr. and Mrs. McMoose refuse to provide any statements to Officer Simon, and both advise that they don't want to file any charges. A neighbor, however, told Officer Simon that she saw Mrs. McMoose hurling her arms near Mr. McMoose's face. Officer Simon:

   A. cannot arrest either Mr. or Mrs. McMoose because neither person wants to file charges

   B. cannot arrest either Mr. or Mrs. McMoose because he didn't witness any assault

   C. may arrest Mrs. McMoose because he has probable cause to believe that she struck her husband

   D. must arrest Mrs. McMoose because there is probable cause to believe that she struck Mr. McMoose and Mr. McMoose has visible signs of injuries

   E. must arrest Mr. McMoose because he is twice the size of Mrs. McMoose, stronger, and obviously provoked her in a verbal argument

2. The following class of people is always protected under the Domestic Violence Act if they are subjected to one of the offenses enumerated in the act:

   A. spouses of the actor
   B. former spouses of the actor
   C. cousins of the actor
   D. all of the above
   E. a and b only

3. Which of the following offenses is *not* considered an act of "domestic violence" under the Domestic Violence Act?

   A. lewdness
   B. harassment
   C. disorderly conduct
   D. all of the above
   E. b and c only

4. Barbie Penn is visiting her cousin Shauna Penn at a park in Parsippany. There, Barbie gets mad at Shauna and bites her in the arm, leaving teeth indentations and a red mark. Parsippany Police Sergeant Mark Combs responds to the scene and witnesses the teeth indentations and red marks on Shauna's arm. Both women deny that anything occurred. Which of the following statements is true?

   A. Without any other facts presented, Officer Combs cannot charge Barbie Penn with simple assault because he did not witness the assault.
   B. Pursuant to the Domestic Violence Act, Officer Combs could arrest Barbie Penn upon a finding of probable cause that a simple assault occurred.
   C. Under the Domestic Violence Act, Officer Combs must arrest Barbie Penn because he witnessed visible signs of injury to Shauna Penn.
   D. Officer Combs should charge Barbie Penn with aggravated assault because biting Shauna exceeds a simple assault.
   E. none of the above

5. During a craps game in Atlantic City, Jessica becomes enraged at her roommate Candy and burns her with her cigarette as she is yelling at her. It was obvious, though, that the burning was accidental. Atlantic City officers, who witnessed the incident, should:

   A. arrest Jessica because Candy is her roommate and there were visible signs of injuries to her
   B. arrest Jessica because they witnessed the injuries
   C. not arrest Jessica because there was not probable cause to believe a simple assault occurred since the burning was accidental
   D. all of the above
   E. a and b only

6. Shrewsbury Patrolman Elliot Sarmucci arrives at a park, responding to an anonymous call about a verbal dispute. When he arrived, he found Bob and Mike yelling at each other, cursing included. Mike had a scratch across the bridge of his nose and was bleeding slightly. After a brief discussion, Patrolman Sarmucci learned that Mike and Bob were lovers who lived together in Bergen County. Which of the following is correct?

   A. Patrolman Sarmucci should advise Mike that he can file a complaint against Bob for simple assault, but the officer cannot arrest Bob because he did not witness the act.
   B. Patrolman Sarmucci could normally arrest Bob under the Domestic Violence Act but can't because Bob lives out of the county.
   C. Patrolman Sarmucci cannot arrest Bob under the Domestic Violence Act because the Act applies only to heterosexuals in a dating relationship.
   D. all of the above
   E. Patrolman Sarmucci must arrest Bob under the Domestic Violence Act.

7. Maggie once dated Arnold, who owns an auto body shop in Cranbury. A year after they break up, Maggie visits Arnold's shop for a tune-up and steals a wrench, valued at $50, from him. Arnold tells Sergeant Prost of the theft. Which of the following statements is true?

   A. Sgt. Prost must arrest Maggie under the Domestic Violence Act because she was once in a dating relationship with Arnold.

   B. Sgt. Prost must arrest Maggie if he has probable cause to believe that she stole the wrench from Arnold.

   C. A disorderly persons offense of theft is not an offense covered under the Domestic Violence Act, so Sgt. Prost does not have to arrest Maggie.

   D. Arnold can file a theft charge against Maggie if he wishes.

   E. c and d

27

Bribery and Corrupt Influence

The following fact pattern pertains to Questions 1 and 2.

Kingman, an electrician, pays Seaver, an employee of a supermarket chain, $5,000 to lobby the supermarket's president to give the chain's electrical contract to Kingman. Kingman also pays Koosman, the mayor of Bridgewater, $7,500 to ensure the passage of a town ordinance that will help Kingman's company grow.

1. In accepting the $5,000 payment, Seaver is guilty of:

   A. a second degree bribery because of the value of the benefit he received
   B. a second degree bribery only if Kingman actually received the contract from the supermarket chain
   C. a third degree bribery because Seaver was the offeree, not the offerer
   D. a fourth degree bribery because Seaver was the offeree, not the offerer
   E. Seaver is not guilty of bribery because a public servant was not involved in the matter.

2. Kingman's payment of $7,500 to Mayor Koosman renders:

   A. Mayor Koosman guilty of second degree bribery
   B. Kingman guilty of second degree bribery
   C. Seaver guilty of second degree bribery
   D. all of the above
   E. a and b only

3. Weinstein, an immigrant from Wales, sweeps the floor of the municipal building in Woodbridge. Newly elected councilman McAllister tells Weinstein that if he polishes McAllister's toenails for seven consecutive weeks, McAllister will vote for an ordinance giving him an extra week vacation. Weinstein agrees. Is McAllister guilty of an offense?

   A. Yes, McAllister is guilty of bribery because McAllister, a councilperson, solicited a benefit from Weinstein in exchange for McAllister's exercise of a vote.
   B. Yes, McAllister is guilty of forgery because his vote would amount to a false writing.
   C. no, because there was no exchange of money
   D. no, because Weinstein, although a government custodian, is not an elected official
   E. a and b

4. Ewing Mayor Winstrol tells newly appointed Ewing Police Director Francis Pinkerton, "I assume you appreciate my appointment of you. Now how about helping out your old friend? I don't need any cash. Just put up my son in your hotel for the next year for free. . . . You promised you would do this if I ensured your appointment." The police director then gives the mayor's son a free room for a year. Could anyone be charged with a crime?

A. no, because the mayor's son was given free room and board *after* the police director was appointed

B. no, because the mayor's *son* received the benefit, not the mayor himself

C. no, because no actual money was exchanged

D. yes, because a benefit provided to a public servant (regardless of whether the public servant is the actual beneficiary himself), even for past official behavior, is criminally actionable if the benefit was received in violation of his official duties

E. yes, because the mayor and police director were personal friends

5. Which of the following acts is illegal?

   A. Fisk, the Marlboro building inspector, issues a permit to Knowles in exchange for a Cross pen set and a cup of chocolate mousse. Knowles never should have received the permit.

   B. Yastremski, the Keansburg property maintenance director, ignores a yard cluttered with an amount of debris that violates town ordinances because the property owner gives him tickets to a Newark Bears baseball game.

   C. Scott, a Camden fire official, issues a summons to Bernard for a burned-out shed. Scott does this although Bernard does not own the shed, have control over it, or is otherwise responsible for it in any way. Scott issues the summons instead because Sharanda, a hooker who hates Bernard, offers Scott sex in exchange for issuing the summons to Bernard.

   D. all of the above

   E. none of the above

6. Under the bribery statute, which of the following is true?

   A. A benefit offered, conferred, or solicited that is of the value of $10,000 or less is a third degree crime.

   B. A benefit offered, conferred, or solicited that is of the value of $75,000 or more is a first degree crime.

   C. A benefit offered, conferred, or solicited that is of the value of $200 or less is a third degree crime.

   D. a and b

   E. b and c

7. Renard Bendini, a State Assemblyman with an eleventh grade education, receives a free trip to Seaside Heights from Mr. Mogul, an insurance company owner. A year later, Assemblyman Renard Bendini votes to give Mr. Mogul's company a state contract. Should Assemblyman Renard Bendini be charged with an offense?

   A. no, because under the "Deprived Educational Resources Act of 1977," Assemblyman Renard Bendini is exempt from criminal prosecution

   B. yes, if Assemblyman Renard Bendini knowingly accepted the vacation in exchange for his vote

   C. yes, if Assemblyman Renard Bendini at least recklessly accepted the vacation while aware that legislation was pending that could benefit Mr. Mogul's insurance company

   D. yes, if Assemblyman Renard Bendini was an immediate family member of Mr. Mogul

   E. c and d

Perjury and Other Falsification in Official Matters

1. A conviction of perjury requires which of the following elements to be present in the defendant's actions?

   A. making a false statement under oath
   B. knowing that the statement is false
   C. having the false statement be "material" to the proceedings
   D. all of the above
   E. a and b only

2. Skip manufactured fake mayonnaise and sold it to several delicatessens in South Jersey. He eventually was caught and charged appropriately. Just before his trial, he threatened to bust a 5-pound jar of nutmeg over Oscar's head if Oscar testified against him. Skip could be charged with?

   A. a disorderly persons offense of aggravated assault
   B. a fifth degree crime of tampering with a witness
   C. a second degree crime of tampering with a witness
   D. a and b
   E. a and c

3. If Skip had never threatened Oscar before he testified but instead hit Oscar in the head with the jar of nutmeg *after* the trial in retaliation for Oscar's testimony against him, Skip would be guilty of:

    A. a disorderly persons offense of simple assault if the striking caused only bodily injury to Oscar
    B. a second degree aggravated assault if the striking caused serious bodily injury to Oscar
    C. a fourth degree crime for witness retaliation
    D. all of the above
    E. none of the above

4. Which of the following actors has committed a disorderly persons offense for impersonating a public servant?

    A. Maxwell, at a masquerade party, pretends to be George W. Bush, President of the United States.
    B. Gloria tells the members of the Argyle Club that she is the CEO of Chrysler and advises that if any members give her $1,000, she will lease them any Chrysler they want for $50 per month.
    C. Sergio impersonates the mayor of Newark in an effort to get sanitation workers to pick up rubbish from an unsightly construction site on the street where he resides.
    D. a and b
    E. a and c

5. Lacey Campbell told Trenton Police that City Councilman Mario Conti was growing marijuana in his backyard. She told police this although she knew her statement was false. What is the *best* offense with which to charge Campbell?

    A. a fourth degree crime for falsely incriminating another
    B. a first degree crime for falsely incriminating another
    C. a fourth degree crime of obstruction of justice
    D. a disorderly persons offense for filing a false police report
    E. New Jersey completely stinks because there is no offense that covers Lacey's despicable act.

6. Simeone is on trial for murder. Horowitz testifies that Simeone was with him at the Super Bowl at the time of the murder, thus giving Simeone an alibi. The prosecution later produces a witness who testifies that Horowitz was indeed lying because Horowitz was at the hospital at the time of the murder. This is the only evidence the prosecution has to show that Horowitz lied on the witness stand. Horowitz could be charged with what offense?

    A. perjury
    B. false swearing
    C. unsworn falsification
    D. false incrimination
    E. no offense at all because the proof of Horowitz's false statement rested upon one witness's contradictory testimony

7. The difference between perjury and false swearing is that:

   A. perjury is a crime of the third degree, but false swearing is a crime of the fourth degree
   B. perjury requires that the false statement must be "material" to the proceedings, but false swearing does not
   C. perjury requires that the defendant not believe that his statement is true, but false swearing does not.
   D. a and b
   E. a and c

8. Karla's house falls victim to a burglar who enters the home by kicking down the front door. Frank orally tells police that he saw a woman in a yellow hat kick down the door. Frank's statement is a lie because he was in Montana at the time of the alleged event. Frank is guilty of what offense?

   A. perjury, a crime of the third degree
   B. false swearing, a crime of the fourth degree
   C. unsworn falsification, a crime of the fourth degree
   D. making a fictitious police report, a disorderly persons offense
   E. no offense at all because people unfortunately can lie

9. Knockwurst applies for the job of Point Pleasant Business Administrator, providing his application to the mayor. On Knockwurst's written application, he states that he previously served as business administrator in three towns in Ohio. Knockwurst never served as a business administrator in any town, Ohio or otherwise. Knockwurst is guilty of what offense?

   A. no offense at all because he did not make his statements under oath
   B. false swearing, a fourth degree crime, if the mayor adopted Knockwurst's application at a joint-unified meeting of the town's electorate
   C. perjury, a third degree crime if the mayor relied on Knockwurst's application in an authorized town council meeting
   D. unsworn falsification, a fourth degree crime, if his application had a notice on it, authorized by law, stating that false statements made on it are punishable
   E. b, c, and d

10. Marcy testifies under oath at a grand jury proceeding that she saw the defendant, Sampson, break the window of Kackie's house and enter her home. The grand jury's role is to decide whether or not to indict Sampson for burglary and aggravated sexual assault. It turns out that Marcy lied; she never saw Sampson do anything. Which of the following statements is true?

   A. Marcy cannot be charged with perjury because a perjury charge is not permitted when false statements are made at grand jury proceedings.
   B. Marcy can be charged only with false swearing.
   C. Marcy has an affirmative defense to a perjury charge if she retracted her false statement during the same grand jury proceedings and her false statement did not cause irreparable harm to Sampson.
   D. all of the above
   E. a and b only

29

Obstructing Governmental Operations: Escapes

The following fact pattern pertains to Questions 1 and 2.

Cecelia Swan, a fugitive, sped past a Hillsdale police officer in her Chevy dump truck. The officer activated the overhead lights and siren of his police cruiser, clearly signaling Swan to stop. Swan ignored the officer's commands and continued to flee. Eventually, after running a red light and two stop signs, Swan plowed into another moving motor vehicle.

1. The *best* offense to charge Swan with for her refusal to stop her vehicle when signaled to do so by Hillsdale Police is:

    A. hindering apprehension
    B. eluding
    C. resisting arrest
    D. obstruction of justice
    E. disorderly conduct

2. The degree of Cecelia Swan's above offense is:

    A. second degree
    B. third degree
    C. fourth degree
    D. disorderly persons offense
    E. petty disorderly persons offense

3. A person under official detention can be charged with escape when:

   A. he leaves a jail without lawful authority
   B. he leaves a prison without lawful authority
   C. he fails to return to prison after being granted a temporary leave
   D. all of the above
   E. a and b only

4. Which of the following statements is true?

   A. A person who absconds parole by leaving the state with the purpose of avoiding supervision is liable for administrative repercussions but has not committed a criminal offense.
   B. Absconding parole means that the defendant has complied with all supervisory mandates and has completed his parole requirements.
   C. A person who has absconded parole by going into hiding with the purpose of avoiding supervision has committed a third degree crime.
   D. Absconding parole means that the defendant has violated his probation status and is now being placed on parole.
   E. none of the above

5. Which of the following actions constitutes hindering apprehension?

   A. Peter knows that the police are seeking to arrest Cecelia for burglary. He purposely hides her in his closet when the police come to his house looking for her.
   B. Archie knows Lois has skipped bail on drug charges. He gives Lois a blond wig, nose ring, and collagen for her lips in order for her to disguise her appearance.
   C. Morris gives Frankie $1,000 for airfare to help Morris get out of the country so he can avoid conviction in his upcoming sexual assault trial.
   D. all of the above
   E. none of the above because a person can't be convicted of hindering *another's* apprehension

6. Tomas is being chased by police officers with trained canines. To avoid being captured, Tomas viciously kills one of the dogs. For killing the dog, Tomas is guilty of:

   A. a first degree crime
   B. although it should be a first degree crime, a third degree crime
   C. although it should be a first degree crime, a disorderly persons offense
   D. as ridiculous as it sounds, he is liable only in a civil matter
   E. *res ipsa loquitor*

7. A juror in the criminal trial of Mark Garner attempts to sell her knowledge of Garner's case to a film production company. Which of the following statements is true?

   A. The juror is guilty of a fourth degree crime if she attempted to make the sale during the trial.
   B. The juror is guilty of a fourth degree crime if she attempted to make the sale after the trial concluded but before the jury rendered the verdict.
   C. The juror is guilty of no offense at all if she attempted to make the sale after her service as a juror was terminated.
   D. all of the above
   E. a and c only

The following fact pattern pertains to Questions 8 and 9.

The wife of Seaside Heights Police Officer Mark Garner had a restraining order issued against him under the New Jersey Domestic Violence Act. Two times Garner violated this judicial order. One, he showed up at his wife's residence, knocked on the door, handed her roses when she answered it, and then left. The second time, as he was driving in his police cruiser, he noticed his wife on her front lawn with another man. Garner stopped his car, ran up to her, slapped her in the face, and left. His wife suffered a slight bruise on her face.

8. Under the facts of the second case, when he slapped his wife in the face, Garner is guilty of:

   A. simple assault because she suffered only bodily injury due to the slap
   B. aggravated assault because he struck his wife who was protected under a restraining order
   C. fourth degree contempt because the conduct constituting the violation of the restraining order constituted an offense
   D. no offense, because he was on duty and acting under the color of law
   E. a and c

9. Under the facts of the first case, when he gave her roses and left, Garner is guilty of:

    A. a disorderly persons offense of contempt because he violated the restraining order but did not commit any other offense while violating it
    B. a fourth degree contempt because contempt of a restraining order is always a crime of the fourth degree
    C. a second degree contempt because contempt of a restraining order is always a crime of the second degree
    D. simple assault for annoying his wife
    E. no offense at all, as Garner simply showed up at his wife's residence with roses. In order to be guilty of contempt, there must be an underlying offense

10. Which of the following statements is accurate?

    A. Marjorie refused to allow a Summit police officer to effectuate a lawful arrest by clinging to a pole. This is a third degree crime of resisting arrest.
    B. Axel ran from a Wall police officer as the officer was trying to lawfully arrest him for burglary. This constitutes a second degree eluding.
    C. Jamaal threatens to stab a Clifton police officer and flails his arms, all in an effort to prevent the officer from lawfully arresting him on theft charges. This is a third degree crime of resisting arrest.
    D. Erin bites a Glassboro police officer as he's trying to lawfully arrest her for cocaine possession. She then runs from the officer. This constitutes a disorderly persons offense of resisting arrest.
    E. all of the above

Misconduct in Office: Abuse of Office

1. Seaside Heights Police Sergeant Mark Garner entered the evidence locker of his department and stole 50 pounds of seized marijuana. Garner then sold the marijuana to a drug dealer for $10,000 cash and $1,000 worth of cocaine. The *best* offense to charge Garner with is:

   A. contempt
   B. bribery
   C. official deprivation of civil rights
   D. official misconduct
   E. obstruction of justice

2. During patrol, Clint the cop watches nine cars pass him by; some are speeding, and others are driving within the speed limit. Clint does nothing but smile, wave, and play a handheld video game. A tenth car approaches, which Clint pulls over and issues the driver a ticket for speeding. Clint has committed the crime of official deprivation of civil rights in which of the following circumstances?

  A. Clint issued the speeding ticket only because the driver was Italian, not because he was actually speeding.
  B. Although the driver was speeding, Clint would not have issued the speeding ticket but he did because the driver, a male, had long hair and looked like a hippie to Clint.
  C. Clint pulled the driver over and issued him a ticket although the driver was not speeding because "the driver was clearly gay."
  D. all of the above
  E. a and c only

3. Which of the following statements is true about the crime of official deprivation of civil rights?

  A. It is generally a disorderly persons offense.
  B. It is elevated to a crime of the first degree when a public servant commits the crime of murder or kidnapping while violating the provisions of the statute.
  C. This crime applies only to the elderly.
  D. The crime applies only to those protected under the Domestic Violence Act.
  E. This crime protects only public servants.

4. In an effort to hire more teachers (some of whom were his own family members) and to obtain high-tech computer hardware and upgraded athletic equipment, Seaside Heights Superintendent of Schools Herman Diaz ordered monetary disbursements that he knew exceeded the Board of Education's budget. Diaz is guilty of:

   A. a petty disorderly persons offense
   B. a fourth degree crime
   C. a first degree crime
   D. a high crime
   E. no offense at all; he would just be removed as school superintendent

5. Sheriff's Officer Penelope smuggles 10 pounds of cocaine into the jail where she works in an effort to sell it to the jail population. In a separate incident, as an act of revenge, she falsely charges an inmate with prostitution. Is Sheriff's Officer Penelope guilty of the crime of pattern of official misconduct?

   A. no, because sheriff's officers are exempt from the public servant requirement of the statute
   B. no, because in order to be convicted of the crime of a "pattern of misconduct," the criminal acts must be part of a common scheme, not separate, different types of acts
   C. no, because of the doctrine of merger
   D. yes, because she committed at least two acts of official misconduct
   E. yes, because sheriff's officers may carry a gun

6. The crime of pattern of official misconduct is:

   A. a first degree crime
   B. a second degree crime
   C. a third degree crime
   D. It could be a or b.
   E. It could be b or c.

7. In order for a public servant to be convicted of the crime of official deprivation of civil rights, among other elements, he must purposely act to intimidate or discriminate against an individual or group of individuals based on:

    A. anger
    B. greed
    C. race, color, religion, gender, handicap, sexual orientation, or ethnicity
    D. only race color, religion, or ethnicity
    E. all of the above plus age

8. Official misconduct is an offense that applies to:

    A. state assembly member
    B. police officers
    C. judges
    D. firefighters
    E. all of the above

Riot, Disorderly Conduct, and Related Offenses

The following fact pattern pertains to Questions 1 and 2.

At Parson's bar, Juice becomes angry at Parsons and shoves Parsons backward. Parsons is not injured in any way, but yells to Juice, "I'm going to kill you." Parsons then rushes to behind his bar where Juice knows that he keeps a pistol. The entire event was witnessed by a Lyndhurst police officer, who grabbed Parsons just as he got to the back of the bar. A gun was not recovered.

1. What is the *best* offense with which the Lyndhurst police officer to charge Juice?

   A. aggravated assault
   B. simple assault
   C. harassment
   D. disorderly conduct
   E. terroristic threats

2. What is the *best* offense with which the Lyndhurst police officer to charge Parsons?

   A. aggravated assault
   B. simple assault
   C. harassment
   D. disorderly conduct
   E. terroristic threats

3. Harassment is elevated to a crime of the fourth degree when:

   A. there are more than 10 acts of alarming conduct that constitute the pattern of harassment
   B. there are more than 25 acts of alarming conduct that constitute the pattern of harassment.
   C. the act(s) of harassment occur after 2:00 A.M.
   D. the defendant commits the act(s) of harassment while on probation or parole as a result of a conviction of an indictable offense
   E. Harassment is never a crime of the fourth degree but is always a disorderly persons offense.

4. Arriving in the town of Glen Rock with a special electric saw, The Brainiac cut out a piece of the town's "rock." What is the *best* offense with which to charge The Brainiac?

   A. maintaining a nuisance under 2C:33-12
   B. desecration of venerated objects under 2C:33-9
   C. abating a nuisance under 2C:33-12.1
   D. disorderly conduct under 2C:33-2
   E. harassment under 2C:33-4

5. The Brainiac's offense as described above is:

   A. a petty disorderly persons offense
   B. a disorderly persons offense
   C. a crime of the third degree
   D. a crime of the first degree
   E. adjudicated only in juvenile court

6. The crime of riot encompasses what separate offense as one of its elements?

   A. simple assault
   B. disorderly conduct
   C. harassment
   D. terroristic threats
   E. none of the above

7. The Brainiac wandered through the streets of Newark. On foot, he repeatedly stopped pedestrians and spoke to them. In his pickup truck, he repeatedly circled a two-block area, twice stopping. On each occasion that he stopped, he passed to and received something from the person with whom he was speaking. All of the Brainiac's above-described activities were witnessed by Newark Police Sergeant Michael Stallone. Which of the following statements is true?

   A. Based on the totality of the circumstances, Sergeant Stallone can charge The Brainiac with the disorderly persons offense of loitering to obtain CDS but only because he personally witnessed all of the activities described above.
   B. Based on the totality of the circumstances, Sergeant Stallone can charge The Brainiac with the disorderly persons offense of loitering to obtain CDS, even if he did not personally witness all of the activities described above.
   C. Sergeant Stallone cannot charge The Brainiac with the disorderly persons offense of loitering to obtain CDS based solely on The Brainiac's activities as described above.
   D. Loitering to obtain CDS is not a disorderly persons offense. It's a crime of the first degree.
   E. There is no such offense known as *loitering to obtain CDS*.

8. Marvin entered a grocery store in Springfield and began scream-ing and jumping up and down. He then jumped up on the counter, knocking over all the items on it, and throwing a bottle against the wall. The most appropriate offense to charge Marvin with is what?

   A. disorderly conduct
   B. harassment
   C. terroristic threats
   D. simple assault
   E. riot

9. The Brainiac called his girlfriend at 4:00 A.M., waking her up, just to talk. Annoyed, she hung the phone up on him. The *best* offense to charge The Brainiac with is what?

   A. disorderly conduct
   B. harassment
   C. terroristic threats
   D. stalking
   E. no offense at all

10. A person can be convicted of maintaining a nuisance under which of the following circumstances?

   A. by creating a condition that endangers the safety or health of a considerable number of persons
   B. by maintaining premises where persons gather to engage in unlawful conduct
   C. by maintaining a house of prostitution
   D. all of the above
   E. a and b only

11. The Brainiac smoked a cigarette on a public bus in Paterson. He is guilty of what?

    A. a crime of the first degree for smoking in public
    B. a petty disorderly persons offense for smoking in public
    C. a disorderly persons offense of disorderly conduct
    D. a disorderly persons offense of abating a nuisance
    E. no offense at all

12. The Brainiac threw eggs at a moving bus in Paterson. He is guilty of what?

    A. a disorderly persons offense if no one was injured and no property damage occurred
    B. a fourth degree crime if bodily injury occurred
    C. a fourth degree crime if there was pecuniary loss in excess of $500 but less than $2000
    D. a second degree crime if serious bodily injury occurred
    E. all of the above

13. Knucklehead, age 40, brings a liter of vodka into a public elementary school in Parsippany. Which of the following statements is true?

    A. Knucklehead is guilty of no offense at all if he obtained written permission by the Parsippany School Board of Education to bring the vodka into the elementary school.
    B. Knucklehead is guilty of no offense if he obtained written permission by the elementary school principal to bring the vodka into the elementary school.
    C. Knucklehead is guilty of no offense if he obtained written permission by the Parsippany School Board attorney, under the authority of the School Board, to bring the vodka into the elementary school.
    D. all of the above
    E. Knucklehead is guilty of a disorderly persons offense regardless of who gave him written permission to bring the vodka into the elementary school.

14. "Bob the Drug Dealer" provides cocaine to "Ted the Addict." During this sale, Bob calls a pager to notify his partner, "Mike the Money Man," that the transaction has been completed. The use of the pager device under these circumstances, renders Bob guilty of what?

    A. a petty disorderly persons offense
    B. a fourth degree crime
    C. a first degree crime
    D. a high crime
    E. no offense at all

15. Nicola, a licensed used car dealer, sold a 1986 Chevy Cavalier on a Sunday. Nicola is guilty of what degree offense?

    A. a disorderly persons offense
    B. a fourth degree crime
    C. a first degree crime
    D. an offense of language
    E. no offense at all

16. Costello, 45, consumed two glasses of wine in an Italian restaurant on a Sunday. Costello is guilty of what degree offense?

    A. a disorderly persons offense
    B. a fourth degree crime
    C. a first degree crime
    D. an offense of language
    E. no offense at all

17. The Brainiac called the Kearny Fire Department and reported that an explosion was about to occur at the town's library. The Brainiac is guilty of what?

    A. a third degree crime
    B. a third degree crime only if he knew that his report was false
    C. a petty disorderly persons offense
    D. a petty disorderly persons offense only if he knew that his report was false
    E. a fifth degree crime

18. Disorderly conduct is:

    A. a petty disorderly persons offense
    B. a disorderly persons offense
    C. a first degree crime
    D. any of the above, depending upon the degree of violence involved
    E. a and b only

19. In order to be convicted of a failure to disperse, which of the following elements must be present?

    A. Five or more people must be participating in a course of disorderly conduct.
    B. The conduct must be likely to cause substantial harm.
    C. A peace officer or public servant must order the participants to disperse from the vicinity.
    D. The defendants must refuse or knowingly fail to leave.
    E. all of the above

20. Schmoz showed up at a Hackensack Library Board meeting and locked the members out of the building. Which of the following statements is true?

    A. Schmoz is guilty of a second degree crime for purposely disrupting and preventing this lawful meeting—as long as he used CDS while inside.
    B. Schmoz is guilty of a disorderly persons offense for purposely disrupting and preventing this lawful meeting.
    C. Schmoz has an affirmative defense if he is a member of the Hackensack Library Board.
    D. all of the above
    E. none of the above

21. Political activist Herschel Karrecht publicly argued, via a microphone, that the New Jersey State Supreme Court's *Abbott* decision inappropriately allocated funds to some public school districts while shortchanging others. Camden Police Officer Jeremy Cantbright arrested Karrecht for disorderly conduct in the Camden park where he was making his speech. Which of the following statements best describes the lawfulness of Officer Cantbright's arrest?

    A. Cantbright appropriately charged Karrecht with disorderly conduct because Karrecht used a microphone.

    B. Cantbright appropriately charged Karrecht with disorderly conduct because he disagreed with the State Supreme Court.

    C. Cantbright appropriately charged Karrecht with disorderly conduct because his conduct was indeed disorderly.

    D. Cantbright inappropriately charged Karrecht with disorderly conduct because nothing in the fact pattern indicates that Karrecht did anything more than carry out his First Amendment right to free speech.

    E. Cantbright would have effectuated a lawful arrest of Karrecht for disorderly conduct if Karrecht had committed *res ispa loquitor.*

Public Indecency

1. The clerk of a store known as The Annex sold two sexually explicit magazines to Arthur, age 17. The clerk is guilty of what?

   A. a third degree crime if he "knew" the magazines he was selling to Arthur had "obscene material" in it
   B. a third degree crime regardless of whether he "knew" the magazines he was selling to Arthur had "obscene material" in it
   C. a first degree crime if he was related to Arthur
   D. a and c
   E. b and c

2. The clerk in Question 1 would have an affirmative defense and be guilty of no offense at all if:

   A. Arthur falsely represented "in or by writing" that he was 18
   B. Arthur appeared 18 or older to an ordinary, prudent person
   C. the clerk relied in good faith on Arthur's 18 plus appearance and written representation, thereby actually believing he was 18 or over
   D. All of the above factors are necessary for an affirmative defense.
   E. There is no affirmative defense to selling "obscene material" to a juvenile.

3. Promoting prostitution is most serious—a second degree crime—in which of the following circumstances?

   A. Sarah knowingly promotes the prostitution of her 14-year-old daughter, Jennifer.
   B. Sarah knowingly promotes the prostitution of her unrelated 14-year-old friend, Janice.
   C. Sarah knowingly promotes the prostitution of her adult sister, Melanie.
   D. Promoting prostitution is always a second degree crime except in circumstances of neglect when it becomes a first degree crime.
   E. a and b

4. Sarah has an affirmative defense to promoting prostitution of a minor if:

A. the minor falsely represented "in or by writing" that she was 18

B. the minor appeared 18 or older to an ordinary, prudent person

C. Sarah relied in good faith on the minor's 18 plus appearance and written representation, thereby actually believing she was 18 or older.

D. All of the above factors are necessary for an affirmative defense.

E. There is no affirmative defense to promoting the prostitution of a minor.

5. John, 30, goes to Mack Daddy's house of prostitution and pays Wilma, 21, an employee of Mack Daddy's, $50 to have sex with him. John and Wilma had never met each other before. This is the first offense for both actors. With what should John and Wilma be charged?

A. John should be charged with a disorderly persons offense of engaging in prostitution, and Wilma should be charged with a third degree crime for promoting prostitution.

B. John should be charged with a third degree crime for promoting prostitution, and Wilma should be charged with a disorderly persons offense for engaging in prostitution.

C. Both John and Wilma should be charged with a disorderly persons offense for engaging in prostitution.

D. Both John and Wilma should be charged with a third degree crime for promoting prostitution.

E. Both John and Wilma are two consenting adults and shouldn't be charged with anything.

6. In Question 5, if this was a second offense for Wilma, her charge should be what degree?

   A. first degree
   B. second degree
   C. fourth degree
   D. disorderly persons offense
   E. John and Wilma are two consenting adults, so Wilma shouldn't be charged with any offense at all.

7. In Questions 5 and 6, if Wilma was 15 instead of 21, John would be guilty of what degree offense?

   A. a second degree crime
   B. a third degree crime
   C. a disorderly persons offense
   D. any of the above, depending upon whether Wilma consented and how much she was paid
   E. no offense at all if John had a reasonable, mistaken belief as to her age

8. Babs owns a convenience store in Passaic County. At her store she sells various magazines that contain "obscene material" (standard nudity magazines). An undercover police officer watched Babs sell one of the magazines to a 33-year-old woman. What should Babs be charged with?

   A. nothing because thousands of stores across the state sell "obscene material" to adults
   B. nothing if the town has adopted a municipal ordinance to legally permit the sale of "obscene material"
   C. a fourth degree crime if the town has not adopted a municipal ordinance to legally permit the sale of "obscene material"
   D. b and c
   E. none of the above

9. Bobby has AIDS and has sex with his partner. Is Bobby guilty of an offense?

   A. Yes, he is guilty of a third degree crime if his partner does not know that he has AIDS.
   B. Yes, he is guilty of a disorderly persons offense if his partner does not know that he has AIDS.
   C. No, he is not guilty of any offense if he had informed his partner that he had AIDS and his partner still consented to having sex with him.
   D. b and c
   E. a and c

10. The Brainiac owns and manages Mack Daddy's, a private, 24-hour club purporting to hold an exclusive membership of checkers and jacks players. In reality, Mack Daddy's was a "house of prostitution" where The Brainiac encouraged more than 30 adult employees to have sex with patrons in exchange for money. The Brainiac took 50% of all monies earned by his employees' acts of prostitution. The Brainiac is guilty of what offense?

   A. a third degree crime of engaging in prostitution
   B. a third degree crime of promoting prostitution
   C. a first degree crime of engaging in prostitution
   D. a third degree crime of soliciting prostitution
   E. a disorderly persons offense of loitering for the purpose of engaging in prostitution

11. Rinaldo pays Mona $50 to comb his hair and whisper sexual words to him while she combs away. The event really turned on Rinaldo. Which of the following statements is true?

    A. Mona is guilty of engaging in prostitution because she was paid to engage in a physical encounter that involved sexual dialogue for the purpose of gratifying Rinaldo.
    B. Rinaldo is guilty of engaging in prostitution because he paid Mona to engage in a physical encounter that involved sexual dialogue for the purpose of gratifying himself.
    C. Rinaldo is guilty of promoting prostitution.
    D. a and b
    E. Neither Rinaldo nor Mona is guilty of any act of prostitution.

12. Jimminey Croquet owns a one-room brick building in Carteret. There he brings men to have sex with several different women. The women are paid for their sexual services. Jimminey Croquet, though, does not receive any money from the men or women for their sexual acts. Instead, the women give Jimminey various fruits and a carpet cleaner for bringing them the customers. Jimminey Croquet is guilty of:

    A. promoting prostitution
    B. engaging in prostitution
    C. drafting prostitution
    D. all of the above
    E. none of the above

35

Controlled Dangerous Substance

The following fact pattern pertains to Questions 1–3.

Charlie Chaplowitz maintained a massive heroin distribution center in the lower level of his restaurant, The Fire Down Under, in Hawthorne. In an effort to prevent law enforcement officers (or any other uninvited guests) from entering the facility, Chaplowitz erected two thick, solid steel doors, a comuterized security card system, and a hidden alarm system. Hawthorne Police raided his facility, confiscating more than 500 pounds of heroin, all of which was being prepared and packaged for the purpose of being distributed to buyers.

1. For the 500 pounds of heroin, Hawthorne Police should charge Chaplowitz with what offense?

   A. fourth degree possession of heroin
   B. first degree possession of heroin with intent to distribute it
   C. third degree possession of heroin with intent to distribute it
   D. all of the above, depending upon the packaging
   E. none of the above

2. For installing the steel doors, computerized security system, and hidden alarm system at his distribution center, Chaplowitz is guilty of what offense?

   A. third degree heroin possession
   B. a disorderly persons offense of fortifying a drug distribution center
   C. a third degree crime of fortifying a drug distribution center
   D. a second degree crime of prescription legend drug housing
   E. no offense at all, because steel doors and alarms are not illegal

3. If Chaplowitz had "booby traps" at his drug distribution center, he would be guilty of:

   A. a second degree crime
   B. a third degree crime
   C. a disorderly persons offense
   D. all of the above, depending upon the type of "booby trap"
   E. There is no offense that defines or categorizes "booby traps."

The following fact pattern pertains to Questions 4–6.

Red Beard was arrested after undercover police officers observed him selling 11 ounces of cocaine to buyer Dumb Head. The cocaine was divided into 29 individually wrapped packages marked with the logo "Tuned Up."

4. Red Beard is guilty of what?

    A. only third degree cocaine possession because he sold only 11 ounces of coke
    B. third degree distribution of CDS because the quantity of cocaine exceeded 10 ounces but was less than 1 pound
    C. third degree distribution of CDS because there were between 15 and 30 individually wrapped packages
    D. first degree distribution of CDS because the quantity of cocaine exceeded 5 ounces
    E. b and c

5. If Red Beard conducted his cocaine transaction within 1,000 feet of school property, he should be charged with what?

    A. an additional third degree offense under 2C:35-7
    B. an additional second degree offense under 2C:35-7
    C. an additional first degree offense under 2C:35-7
    D. no additional offense if he was unaware that his drug distribution occurred within 1,000 feet of school property
    E. no additional offense if no juveniles were present on the school property at the time of the drug distribution

6. If Red Beard conducted his cocaine distribution within 500 feet of a public park, he should be charged with what?

    A. an additional third degree offense under 2C:35-7.1
    B. an additional second degree offense under 2C:35-7.1
    C. an additional first degree offense under 2C:35-7.1
    D. no additional offense if he was unaware that his drug distribution occurred within 500 feet of a public park
    E. no additional offense if no juveniles were present at the park at the time of the drug distribution

7. Which of the following statements about possession of CDS with intent to distribute is accurate?

   A. If the CDS is possessed with the intent to distribute within 1,000 feet of a public housing facility, the defendant should be charged with an additional fourth degree crime.

   B. Possession of CDS with the intent to distribute it is a crime one degree less than actual distribution of the CDS.

   C. Possession of 2 ounces of heroin, with the intent to distribute it, is a second degree crime, the same degree crime as if the heroin was actually distributed.

   D. a and b

   E. a and c

The following fact pattern pertains to Questions 8 and 9.

Schwartz has been under surveillance by Upper Saddle River police for six months. Finally, detectives arrange an undercover buy at his home; there, they purchase 75 marijuana plants from him. Once busted, Schwartz rolls on Leroy, arranging a buy of 250 milligrams of LSD. Leroy ultimately sold that amount of LSD to the same detectives.

8. Upper Saddle River police should charge Schwartz with what?

   A. third degree distribution of marijuana because Schwartz cooperated and gave them Leroy

   B. third degree distribution of marijuana because marijuana distribution is always a crime of the third degree

   C. third degree distribution of marijuana because the detectives confiscated less than 100 plants

   D. first degree distribution of marijuana if the plants weighed more than 10 pounds

   E. first degree distribution of marijuana because he sold them 75 plants

9. Upper Saddle River police should charge Leroy with what?

    A. a third degree crime of distributing LSD if he ultimately rolls on another dealer

    B. a third degree crime of distributing LSD because LSD distribution is always a crime of the third degree

    C. a third degree crime of distributing LSD because he sold detectives 200 milligrams or more of LSD

    D. a first degree crime of distributing LSD because he sold detectives 100 milligrams or more of LSD

    E. none of the above

10. Essex County Sheriff's Officer Archie Pitt charges Monte McMartin with possession of 10 ounces of powder cocaine with the intent to distribute it. The 10 ounces is a combination of powder cocaine mixed with a powder dilutant. Which of the following statements is true?

    A. Officer Pitt should charge McMartin with a second degree offense because the quantity he confiscated exceeds 5 ounces. This is regardless of the amount of dilutant that may be involved; the trier of fact will determine the ultimate quantity.

    B. Officer Pitt should charge McMartin with a first degree offense because the quantity he confiscated exceeds 5 ounces. This is regardless of the amount of dilutant that may be involved; the trier of fact will determine the ultimate quantity.

    C. Officer Pitt should charge McMartin with a third degree offense if he is unsure what amount of the 10 ounces is dilutant.

    D. Officer Pitt should charge McMartin with a petty disorderly persons offense.

    E. Officer Pitt should let McMartin go upon a pledge of rehabilitation.

11. Snooty snorts a whole bundle of cocaine and then dies. Which of the following is true?

    A. A dealer who distributed the cocaine to Snooty could be convicted of a first degree crime, held strictly liable for his death.
    B. A friend who dispensed the cocaine to Snooty could be convicted of a first degree crime, held strictly liable for his death.
    C. A dealer who distributed the cocaine to Snooty could not be held strictly liable for his death and convicted of a first degree crime—if Snooty died a year later—after Snooty had inhaled cocaine from several other dealers.
    D. all of the above
    E. a and c only

12. Mark sells Victor 5 pounds of flour for $50,000, purporting it to be cocaine. Victor indeed believes it is cocaine and goes home and begins to snort it. Mark is guilty of what offense?

    A. a first degree distribution of cocaine under 2C:35-5
    B. a first degree distribution of distributing counterfeit cocaine under 2C:35-5
    C. a third degree distribution of imitation cocaine under 2C:35-11
    D. a disorderly persons offense of failure to make lawful disposition under 2C:35-10
    E. none of the above because Mark can't be prosecuted for selling flour

13. Red Beard was caught by Hawthorne Police with a dime bag of marijuana holding under 50 grams. Red Beard is guilty of what offense?

    A. a misdemeanor
    B. a first degree crime
    C. a third degree crime because he had under 50 grams of marijuana, which is the lowest degree offense for CDS possession
    D. a disorderly persons offense because he had under 50 grams of marijuana, which is the lowest degree offense for CDS possession
    E. no offense if he had a note from his principal

14. Imitation CDS is:

    A. the same as counterfeit CDS
    B. oregano purporting to be marijuana
    C. flour purporting to be cocaine
    D. all of the above
    E. b and c only

36

Drug Paraphernalia

1. The following group of items can be considered drug paraphernalia:

    A. pipes, bongs, straws
    B. shoes, sneakers, crumb buns
    C. glass containers, vials, indoor gardening lamps
    D. all of the above
    E. a and c only

2. Possession of drug paraphernalia under 2C:36-2 is:

    A. a crime of the first degree
    B. a crime of the third degree
    C. a disorderly persons offense
    D. all of the above, depending upon the type of paraphernalia
    E. none of the above

3. One who distributes a hash pipe is guilty of what offense?

    A. a crime of the first degree

    B. a crime of the fourth degree

    C. a disorderly persons offense

    D. modus operendi only

    E. *res ipsa loquitor* under the doctrine of connip-
       tions

4. The following persons may legally possess a hypodermic needle:

    A. podiatrists

    B. veterinarians

    C. sharp shooters

    D. all of the above

    E. a and b only

37

Gambling Offenses

1. Which of the following statements is true about a person who participates in an illegal card game only as a player?

   A. He is guilty of only a petty disorderly persons offense.
   B. He is guilty of a fourth degree crime under all circumstances.
   C. He is guilty of an offense one degree less than the actor guilty of promoting the card game.
   D. He is guilty of an offense of the same degree as the actor guilty of promoting the card game.
   E. He has an affirmative defense.

2. Knuckles collects money from losing bettors for an illegal gambling operation. Last week, he received more than $150,000 from losers who made hundreds of bets, pursuant to their understanding that they had to pay up when they lost. Knuckles, a partner in the gambling operation, personally profited from these funds. Knuckles is guilty of what offense for receiving these funds?

   A. nothing, if he was a player himself
   B. a disorderly persons offense because all gambling offenses are now disorderly persons offense
   C. a fourth degree crime of shipboard gambling because of the collection activities
   D. a third degree crime of promoting gambling, given that his $150,000 one-week collection on hundreds of bets exceeded more than five bets totaling more than $1,000 on any given day
   E. a first degree crime of promoting gambling, given that his one-week $150,000 collection on hundreds of bets exceeded more than 50 bets totaling more than $10,000 in any one week

3. Which of the following is *not* an element of the offense in promoting gambling?

   A. The bookmaking must be controlled by organized crime.
   B. The bookmaking must be performed in a centralized location.
   C. The actor must "knowingly engage" in promoting the gambling activities.
   D. all of the above
   E. a and b only

4. The Hyena had authoritative control over the "after-hours" club, The Purple Mule, and ran it. At this club, people played games of poker, blackjack, and craps. The Hyena encouraged the gambling to continue, participated in it, and profited from all players by charging a "playing fee" and by taking in all their monetary losses. Is The Hyena guilty of the offense of maintaining a gambling resort?

   A. yes, because he actively ran the resort, accepted a "playing fee" in exchange for allowing individuals to engage in the illegal games, and profited from their losses
   B. yes, because The Purple Mule was an "after-hours" club, thereby making his club pro rata illegal
   C. no, because the "player fee" permits the arm's-length gambling transactions
   D. no, if The Purple Mule had registered with the municipality as a social club
   E. c and d

5. In order to be convicted of maintaining a gambling resort, the actor must:

   A. receive more than $500 in losses from bettors in any given week
   B. receive more than $500 in losses from bettors in any given day
   C. accept at least five bets and/or receive at least $1,000 in losses from bettors in any given week
   D. accept at least 50 bets and/or receive at least $10,000 in losses from bettors in any given week
   E. none of the above

6. Possessing gambling records is:

   A. a crime of the third degree when the instrument used in a bookmaking scheme reflects more than five bets totaling more than $1,000
   B. a crime of the third degree when the instrument in a lottery scheme reflects more than 100 bets
   C. a disorderly persons offense in all matters other than those described in a and b
   D. all of the above
   E. none of the above—it is always a disorderly persons offense

7. Which of the following does *not* constitute a violation of 2C:37-7 for possession of a gambling device?

   A. Marge possessing five roulette boards at an illegal gambling resort
   B. Mario possessing four decks of playing cards at a card game he holds weekly where he charges a $50 "player fee" for anyone entering the game
   C. Mary possessing seven slot machines at her house that she has for social use
   D. all of the above
   E. none of the above

38

Terrorism

1. Which of the following crimes is *not* a crime that can trigger a conviction of terrorism under 2C:38-2?

   A. kidnapping
   B. murder
   C. criminal restraint
   D. disarming a law enforcement officer
   E. none of the above—all of these offenses can trigger a conviction of terrorism

2. George Evile entered a New Brunswick hotel with a briefcase, placing it in a meeting room with hundreds of political lobbyists. Inside the briefcase was a massive explosive device containing the nerve agent Sarin. The bomb exploded 5 minutes after Evile's departure from the hotel. Fourteen people were killed by the explosion; another 75 were injured. Can Evile be convicted of the crime of terrorism in addition to murder?

   A. no, he can be convicted of either murder or terrorism, but not both
   B. no, if Evile is an American citizen
   C. yes, if he conducted his mass killing to influence the policy of the government by his act of terror
   D. yes, but only if he is an American citizen
   E. c and d

3. Jarrod Mashington is an employee of a medical research facility that is legally performing research on anthrax. Marty Ponroe pays $5,000 to "sneak" him into the building because he "wants to steal $100,000 cash stored in the president's safe." Believing all this, Mashington sneaks Ponroe into the facility where Ponroe steals quantities of anthrax, his true target. Is Mashington guilty of an offense under a *terrorism* statute?

   A. no, but he is guilty of theft and burglary offenses as a co-conspirator
   B. no, because he did not act "purposely" or with "knowledge" that Ponroe was stealing a deadly biological agent
   C. no, because the facility lawfully possessed the anthrax, Mashington was an employee of the facility in lawful possession of the anthrax, and he did not actually steal the anthrax or conspire to do so
   D. yes, because he acted "recklessly" in permitting Ponroe, an unauthorized individual, to access the anthrax
   E. a and b

4. Which of the following is a first degree offense?

   A. unlawfully manufacturing the biological agent, Marberg virus
   B. unlawfully possessing a recombinant molecule vector
   C. threatening to use the biological agent Brucella abortus
   D. all of the above
   E. none of the above, because none of these items exists

5. Hindering the apprehension of a terrorist is:

   A. a first degree crime if the defendant harbored the terrorist, and the terrorist's crime resulted in death
   B. a second degree crime if the defendant provided a disguise for the terrorist, and the terrorist's crime did not result in death
   C. a third degree crime, like any other hindering apprehension charge, if the terrorist's crime did not result in death
   D. a and b
   E. a and c

Firearms, Other Dangerous Weapons, and Instruments of Crime

1. Jermaine, 23, sold handcuffs to Michael, 15. Of what offense is Jermaine guilty?

   A. a first degree weapons trafficking
   B. a third degree weapons distribution
   C. a disorderly persons offense for selling handcuffs to a minor
   D. a civil offense only, to be adjudicated in juvenile court
   E. no offense at all

The following fact pattern pertains to Questions 2 and 3.

Officer Bolognese of the Weehawken Police Department overhears Trumpet tell Sax that he "always carries a baseball bat" in his trunk "just in case a fight breaks out." A couple of months later, Officer Bolognese reports to a dispute by the water. As he's arriving, he sees Trumpet arguing with Woodwin. Trumpet then runs toward his car, popping the trunk with his electronic key. Just as the trunk flies open, Woodwin shoots Trumpet in the leg.

2. Of the following, what is the *best* offense for Officer Bolognese to charge Trumpet with?

   A. no offense at all, because it is not unlawful to possess a baseball bat

   B. no offense at all, because Trumpet was a victim in the matter. He was shot in the leg as he was about to defend himself.

   C. second degree possession of a weapon for unlawful purposes

   D. fifth degree possession of a weapon for unlawful purposes

   E. fourth degree unlawful possession of a weapon

3. Of the following, what is the *best* offense for Officer Bolognese to charge Woodwin with?

   A. second degree possession of a weapon for unlawful purposes

   B. fifth degree possession of a weapon for unlawful purposes

   C. fourth degree unlawful possession of a weapon

   D. a disorderly persons offense if Officer Bolognese learned that Woodwin was an off-duty police officer

   E. no offense at all if Officer Bolognese learned that Trumpet started the dispute

4. Scorpion had been convicted of kidnapping but was "maxed out" and released from prison a completely unsupervised man. Marlboro Police responded to an armed offense in progress at a diner. There, they apprehended Scorpion, who was wielding an automatic rifle at the cashier and patrons as he took all of their cash. He was screaming, "I'll kill you! I'll shoot your heads off!" With which of the following offenses should Marlboro Police charge Scorpion?

   A. robbery, possession of a weapon for unlawful purposes, and an additional fourth degree crime for being a convicted felon in possession of a firearm
   B. burglary, robbery, possession of a weapon for unlawful purposes, and an additional fourth degree crime for being a convicted felon in possession of a firearm
   C. robbery, possession of a weapon for unlawful purposes, and an additional second degree crime for being a convicted felon in possession of a firearm
   D. burglary, robbery, possession of a weapon for unlawful purposes, and an additional second degree crime for being a convicted felon in possession of a firearm
   E. robbery only because all of the other offenses will be merged

5. Scorpion's robbery offense is:

   A. a crime of the first degree because he was armed with a deadly weapon during the course of the robbery
   B. a crime of the first degree because he threatened to kill people during the course of the robbery
   C. a crime of the second degree if the rifle was not loaded
   D. all of the above
   E. a and b only

6. Art Campos, a licensed dealer, delivered a handgun legally purchased by Mike Bimino. Campos is guilty of:

   A. a first degree crime if he delivered the gun to Bimino if it was not being accompanied by a trigger lock or a locked case, gun box container, or other secure facility

   B. a first degree crime only if he "knowingly" delivered the gun to Bimino if it was not being accompanied by a trigger lock or a locked case, gun box container, or other secure facility

   C. a disorderly persons offense if he delivered the gun to Bimino if it was not being accompanied by a trigger lock or a locked case, gun box container, or other secure facility

   D. a disorderly persons offense only if he "knowingly" delivered the gun to Bimino if it was not being accompanied by a trigger lock or a locked case, gun box container, or other secure facility

   E. b and c

7. Welby Marcus, M.D., at his private medical office, treats Weillman for a gunshot wound to his shoulder. Dr. Marcus patches him up and sends him home. Dr. Marcus is guilty of what offense?

   A. no offense at all if he reported the firearm arm wound to law enforcement authorities

   B. a disorderly persons offense if he did not report the firearm wound to law enforcement authorities

   C. a second degree crime if he did not report the firearm wound to law enforcement authorities and a disorderly persons offense for not admitting Weillman to a hospital

   D. a and b

   E. a and c

8. In Hoboken, George Evile sold a kilogram of cocaine to a pawn-broker. During the drug deal, Evile carried a .22 caliber pistol. Which of the following offenses is Evile guilty of violating?

   A. a first degree crime for possession of a weapon for unlawful purposes
   B. a third degree crime for unlawful possession of a weapon
   C. a second degree crime for possession of a firearm during a drug distribution deal
   D. a and c
   E. b and c

9. Sally, angry at her lover Suave for cheating on her with an attorney, shows up at Suave's house with a dagger and attempts to stab him in the neck. Suave, though, wrestles the dagger away from Sally, thwarting her effort. With which of the following offenses could Sally be charged?

   A. a fourth degree crime for unlawfully possessing the dagger
   B. a third degree crime for possession of a weapon for unlawful purposes
   C. attempted murder
   D. all of the above
   E. none of the above

10. Which of the following statements is true?

   A. Possession of a firearm silencer is a fourth degree crime.
   B. Possession of a stun gun is a crime of the fourth degree.
   C. Possession of dum-dum bullets is a crime of the fourth degree.
   D. all of the above
   E. All of the above are disorderly persons offenses.

11. Sal Catanio is an officer in the U.S. Army currently stationed at Fort Dix. After drills one evening, Sal is notified that he is to report, with several other officers of the U.S. armed forces, to Washington, D.C., on a special mission. Sal, pursuant to the orders, loads up an Army vehicle with multiple machine guns and body armor–penetrating bullets. Joining him in the vehicle were 25 other soldiers. En route to Washington, D.C., the Army vehicle breaks down. A state trooper comes to the scene to assist. The state trooper, upon seeing the machine guns and bullets, should charge Sal with what offenses?

    A. unlawful possession of weapons for the machine guns
    B. unlawful possession of body armor–penetrating bullets
    C. possession of a weapon for unlawful purposes
    D. a and b
    E. none of the above because he is exempt for being charged with these offenses

12. In order to be convicted of being the leader of a firearms trafficking network, which of the following elements must be present?

    A. The defendant must conspire with others.
    B. The defendant must unlawfully manufacture, transport, ship, sell, or dispose of any firearm.
    C. The network must exist to earn profit.
    D. all of the above
    E. a and b only

Other Offenses Relating to Public Safety

1. Delta Delta Delta Fraternity brothers Sam Concord and Michael Diaz slapped each fraternity pledge on their backsides with a paddle. The pledges consented to the slapping and received bruises and slight lacerations to their backsides. Concord and Diaz are guilty of which of the following offenses?

   A. third degree aggravated assault
   B. a disorderly persons offense of simple assault
   C. a disorderly persons offense of hazing
   D. a fourth degree crime of aggravated hazing
   E. no offense at all because the bodily harm consented to was not serious

2. Fraternity brother Diaz smacked a paddle against the head of one of the fraternity's pledges, knocking him unconscious and causing him to receive 30 stitches. The pledge consented to the head beating. Diaz could be convicted of what offense(s)?

   A. second degree aggravated assault and fourth degree aggravated hazing

   B. second degree aggravated assault and a disorderly persons offense of hazing

   C. a disorderly persons offense of hazing but no assault charge at all because the pledge consented to the head beating

   D. a fourth degree aggravated hazing but no assault charge at all because the pledge consented to the head beating

   E. aggravated assault only

3. Jugs went to a supermarket, opened a package of cupcakes, spit on the baked goods, and resealed the package. Jugs is guilty of what offense?

   A. a crime of the first degree

   B. a crime of the fourth degree

   C. a petty disorderly persons offense

   D. any of the above, depending on the value of the cupcakes

   E. none of the above

4. Caligula, a pipe-fitter, for some reason decided to remove a stop sign at a busy Union City intersection. On the same day, an unassuming motorist crossed through the intersection without stopping and crashed into a motor vehicle. A passenger in one of the cars was killed. Which of the following statements is accurate?

  A. The driver who passed through the intersection should be charged with vehicular homicide.
  B. The driver who passed through the intersection should not be charged with vehicular homicide but should be charged with a fourth degree negligent homicide if it was proved that he had previously passed through that intersection.
  C. Caligula should be charged with a crime of the second degree.
  D. a and c
  E. b and c

5. Marquis drives on the revoked list in violation of 39:3-40 and gets into an automobile accident. Which of the following statements is *not* true?

  A. If someone was killed during this accident, Marquis could be convicted of a third degree crime.
  B. If someone suffered serious bodily injury during this accident, Marquis could be convicted of a fourth degree crime.
  C. If someone was killed in the accident—and that deceased person acted negligently or recklessly in causing the accident—Marquis would have an affirmative defense and should not be charged with any offense.
  D. If no one was killed or injured in the accident, Marquis could not be convicted of a third or fourth degree crime.
  E. none of the above, because all of the statements are true

1. Veale, a chiropractor, sends out 50 notices to victims of a recent bus crash, soliciting their business—to "help them with back, neck, and other problems that occurred in their August 1, 2005 bus crash on the New Jersey Turnpike." With what offense can Veale be charged?

   A. none because there is nothing unlawful about soliciting patients

   B. a petty disorderly persons offense but only if the solicitation occurred within 30 days after the date of the accident

   C. a petty disorderly persons offense but only if the solicitation occurred within 30 days after the date of the accident and if Veale acted with intent to accept money or something of value for his services

   D. a third degree crime but only if the solicitation occurred within 30 days after the date of the accident and if Veale acted with intent to accept money or something of value for his services

   E. a first degree crime—period

2. Which of the following statements is true?

   A. An employer who fires an employee for "wearing a dress that is too short" is guilty of a disorderly persons offense.
   B. An employer who fires an employee "because the employee doesn't get along well with post office workers" is guilty of a disorderly persons offense.
   C. An employer who fires an employee "because the employee's earnings have been subjected to garnishment" is guilty of a disorderly persons offense.
   D. all of the above
   E. none of the above

3. In which of the following circumstances has a disorderly persons offense *not* been committed?

   A. A pawnbroker required two employees to submit to lie detector tests before hiring them.
   B. A sales executive in the tile business required a female junior salesperson to submit to a lie detector test if she desired continued employment.
   C. The CEO of a leading pharmaceutical company that manufactures CDS requires her employees involved in the CDS manufacturing to submit to lie detector tests before hiring them.
   D. all of the above
   E. a and b only

Racketeering

1. Which of the following "pattern of racketeering" activities can elevate a charge of racketeering to a first degree crime?

   A. activities that involve a crime of violence
   B. activities that involve a crime of the first degree
   C. activities that involve firearms
   D. all of the above
   E. a and b only

2. "Racketeering activity" does *not* include which of the following offenses?

   A. criminal usury
   B. criminal restraint
   C. extortion
   D. burglary
   E. bribery

The following fact pattern pertains to Questions 3 and 4.

George Evile set up an unlawful machine gun manufacturing shop in Jersey City in which he provided and sold in excess of 1,000 machine guns. Evile's purpose in creating the shop was to sell the machine guns in order to raise funds for his terrorist group, MIFA. More than 200 distinct transactions to nearly 150 separate buyers occurred over an eight-year period, the first occurring in 1995. Evile closely monitored his firearms shop, visiting the establishment on a daily basis and barking orders and directives to the dozens of employees who worked for him. When George couldn't make it to the shop, his brother Alex operated the business in his stead.

3. Which of the following facts helps establish that the Evile brothers engaged in a "pattern of racketeering"?

   A. They engaged in more than two incidents of racketeering—more than 200, to be specific.
   B. The incidents began in 1995 and all happened within eight years of each other.
   C. Their racketeering incidents provided a pattern of conduct that had similar purposes, participants, and methods of commission.
   D. all of the above
   E. b and c only

4. In order to ultimately be convicted of racketeering, the Evile brothers must:

   A. engage in a pattern of racketeering activity
   B. be principals in the pattern of racketeering activity
   C. use or invest income, derived from the pattern of racketeering, to acquire an interest in an enterprise whose activities affect trade or commerce
   D. all of the above
   E. a and b only

Answer Key

CHAPTER 1

1. d (2C:1-6)
2. c (2C:1-13)
3. c (2C:1-13)
4. d (2C:1-3)
5. b (2C:1-3)
6. b (2C:1-4)
7. c (2C:1-6)
8. d (2C:1-6)
9. c (2C:1-4)
10. b (2C:1-6)
11. d (2C:1-4)
12. c (2C:1-4)
13. d (2C:1-14)
14. d (2C:1-4)

CHAPTER 2

1. d (2C:2-1)
2. d (2C:2-7)
3. c (2C:2-6)
4. c (2C:2-10, 2C:2-4, 2C:2-8)
5. e (2C:2-9)
6. b (2C:2-10)
7. c (2C:2-4)
8. d (2C:2-12)

CHAPTER 3

1. c (2C:3-4)
2. c (2C:3-6)

3. d (2C:3-4)
4. d (2C:3-7)

CHAPTER 4

1. e (2C:4-1)

CHAPTER 5

1. d (2C:5-1)
2. a (2C:5-2)
3. b (2C:5-4)
4. b (2C:5-5)
5. e (2C:5-4)
6. c (2C:5-4,
       2C:20-2b.(2))
7. a (2C:5-2g.)
8. a (2C:5-2)
9. c (2C:5-2)
10. e (2C:5-2b.)
11. a (2C:5-4)
12. b (2C:5-4)

CHAPTER 7

1. d (2C:7-2b.(1) & (2))
2. e (2C:7-2b.(2), 2C:13-6)
3. d (2C:7-2a.(2))
4. a (2C:7-2b.(2))
5. d (2C:7-2)

CHAPTER 11

1. b (2C:11-2)
2. c (2C:11-4)
3. a (2C:11-3)
4. a (2C:11-4)
5. c (2C:11-3)
6. e (2C:11-4)
7. b (2C:11-4)
8. c (2C:11-3)
9. e (2C:11-5b.(3))
10. d (2C:11-6)
11. c (2C:11-5.1)
12. b (2C:11-3a.(3))
13. c (2C:11-4b.(2))
14. d (2C:11-3a.(1) & (2))
15. c (2C:11-3)
16. a (2C:11-3a.(3))
17. d (2C:11-3a.(3))
18. b (2C:11-4a.(2))
19. d (2C:11-6)
20. d (2C:11-3a.(1) or (2))
21. a (2C:11-5)
22. d (2C:11-3a.(1) & (2))
23. c (2C:11-4a.)
24. e (2C:11-2)
25. c (2C:11-6)

CHAPTER 12

1. b (2C:12-1a.)
2. c (2C:12-1b.(9))

3. d (2C:12-1b.(4))
4. b (2C:12-1b.(1) and 2C:12-1b.(11))
5. d (2C:12-1b.(11))
6. a (2C:12-3)
7. e (2C:12-11)
8. a (2C:12-1b.(5)(a))
9. a (2C:12-1b.(5)(f))
10. c (2C:12-1.2)
11. e (2C:12-1f.)
12. d (2C:12-1b.(1)(2)&(3))
13. a (2C:12-13)
14. d (2C:12-13)
15. b (2C:12-1a. & b.)
16. e (2C:12-2)
17. e (2C:12-3)
18. a (2C:12-1b.(2))
19. c (2C:12-11)
20. d (2C:11-3)
21. b (2C:12-10)
22. b (2C:12-1b.(10))
23. c (2C:12-1b.(9))
24. b (2C:12-1b.(4))
25. d (2C:12-10)
26. e (2C:12-10b.)
27. d (2C:12-10c., d., e.)
28. a (2C:12-10b.)
29. e (2C:2-10b.(2))
30. d (2C:12-1a.(3))
31. d (2C:12-1b.(4) & (10))
32. c (2C:33-4)
33. e (2C:12-1)

CHAPTER 13

1. b (2C:13-3)
2. a (2C:13-5)
3. e (2C:13-1)
4. a (2C:13-2)
5. d (2C:13-1)
6. c (2C:13-1)
7. a (2C:13-1c.)
8. c (2C:13-4, 2C:13-1b.(4))
9. d (2C:13-1e.(3))
10. d (2C:13-6)
11. e (2C:13-3)

CHAPTER 14

1. a (2C:14-2)
2. a (2C:14-2a.(3))
3. b (2C:14-2c.(1))
4. e (2C:14-4)
5. c (2C:14-9)
6. c (2C:14-2a.)
7. d (2C:14-2a.(1))
8. d (2C:14-3b.)
9. b (2C:14-2b.)
10. d (2C:14-4b.)
11. b (2C:14-9b.)
12. e (2C:11-3, 2C:14-2)
13. b (2C:14-2c.(2))
14. c (2C:14-1)
15. e (2C:14-3)
16. b (2C:14-3)

17. a (2C:14-9b.)
18. b (2C:14-9b.)
19. a (2C:14-4)
20. c (2C:14-2a.(7))
21. e (2C:14-3b., 2C:14-2c.(1) through (4))
22. b (2C:14-3b.)

CHAPTER 15

1. d (2C:15-2)
2. e (2C:15-1a.(3))
3. e (2C:15-2a.(1), (3), & (4); 2C:12-1b.(2))
4. d (2C:15-1a.(1), 2C:15-1b.)
5. d (2C:15-1, 2C:20-2)
6. c (2C:15-2a.)
7. a (2C:15-2b.)

CHAPTER 16

1. e (2C:16-1)
2. d (2C:16-1)
3. c (2C:16-1)
4. e (2C:16-1)
5. a (2C:16-1)
6. e (2C:16-1c.)

CHAPTER 17

1. c (2C:17-3a.(2))
2. a (2C:17-3b.(2))
3. e (2C:17-6)
4. b (2C:17-7)
5. e (2C:17-1a.(1) & (2), 2C:12-1b.(1))
6. d (2C:17-3b.)
7. b (2C:17-1b.(1) & (2), 2C:18-1)
8. c (2C:17-3b.)
9. b (2C:17-1c.(2))
10. a (2C:17-1a.(2))
11. d (2C:17-2a.(1) & 2C:17-1b.(2))
12. a (2C:17-2a.(1))
13. e (2C:17-1a. & b.)
14. c (2C:17-1b.(5))
15. b (2C:17-1d.)
16. c (2C:17-3.1)
17. c (2C:17-3.1)
18. d (2C:17-1a.(1), 2C:17-2a.(1), 2C:17-8)
19. d (2C:17-3b.(6))

CHAPTER 18

1. b (2C:18-2a.(1))
2. c (2C:18-2)
3. a (2C:18-3b.(2))
4. d (2C:18-2b.(1))
5. e (2C:18-3c., 2C:18-3d.(3))
6. d (2C:18-2c.(1))

CHAPTER 20

1. b   (2C:20-2)
2. d   (2C:20-2b.(1)(a), (c) & (e))
3. e   (2C:20-18, 2C:20-7.1)
4. c   (2C:20-11)
5. c   (2C:20-11c.(2))
6. d   (2C:20-7a. & b.)
7. b   (2C:20-2b.(1))
8. a   (2C:20-7.1)
9. b   (2C:20-10d.)
10. d   (2C:20-6)
11. c   (2C:20-36)
12. d   (2C:20-9, 2C:20-2b.(2))
13. d   (2C:20-5)
14. e   (2C:20-5, 2C:20-2b.(1)(b))
15. b   (2C:20-4)
16. c   (2C:20-2b.(2)(a))

CHAPTER 21

1. b   (2C:21-2)
2. e   (2C:21-32)
3. e   (2C:21-10)
4. d   (2C:21-17.3)
5. d   (2C:21-4)
6. b   (2C:21-1)
7. b   (2C:21-1)
8. d   (2C:21-2.2)
9. a   (2C:21-2.2)

10. d   (2C:21-13)
11. a   (2C:21-18)
12. c   (2C:21-1a.(1))
13. b   (2C:21-11a. & 2C:21-11c.)
14. d   (2C:21-11d.)
15. c   (2C:21-25b.(2)(a))
16. a   (2C:21-27a.)
17. b   (2C:21-22)
18. e   (2C:21-19a.(2))
19. a   (2C:21-19b.)
20. e   (2C:21-5)
21. c   (2C:21-5b.)

CHAPTER 22

1. e   (2C:22-1a. & b.)

CHAPTER 24

1. d   (2C:24-4b.(5)(b) & 2C:24-4b.(5)(a))
2. c   (2C:24-9b.)
3. d   (2C:24-9d.)
4. a   (2C:24-8a.)
5. c   (2C:24-7)
6. b   (2C:24-4b.(4))
7. d   (2C:24-4b.(4))
8. a   (2C:24-4b.(3))
9. b   (2C:24-4b.(5)(a))
10. e   (2C:24-4a.)
11. c   (2C:24-4a.)

CHAPTER 25

1. d   (2C:25-21a.(1))
2. e   (2C:25-19d.)
3. c   (2C:25-19a.)
4. a   (2C:25-19d.)
5. c   (2C:25-21a.)
6. e   (2C:25-21a.)
7. e   (2C:25-21a.)

CHAPTER 27

1. e   (2C:27-2)
2. e   (2C:27-2)
3. a   (2C:27-2a.)
4. d   (2C:27-4a.(1))
5. d   (2C:27-10a. & b., 2C:27-11a. & b.)
6. c   (2C:27-2)
7. b   (2C:27-4a.(1), 2C:27-10a.)

CHAPTER 28

1. d   (2C:28-1)
2. c   (2C:28-5a.)
3. d   (2C:28-5b., 2C:12-1c.(1) & (3), 2C:12-1b.(1) & (2), 2C:12-1b.(11))
4. c   (2C:28-8a.)
5. a   (2C:28-4a.)
6. e   (2C:28-1e.)
7. d   (2C:28-1a., 2C:28-2a.)

8. d   (2C:28-4b.(2))
9. d   (2C:28-3a.)
10. c   (2C:28-1d.)

CHAPTER 29

1. b   (2C:29-2b.)
2. a   (2C:29-2b.)
3. d   (2C:29-5a.)
4. c   (2C:29-5b.)
5. d   (2C:29-3a.(1)-(7))
6. b   (2C:29-3.1)
7. d   (2C:29-8.1a.)
8. e   (2C:12-1a.(1), 2C:29-9b.)
9. a   (2C:29-9b.)
10. c   (2C:29-2a.(1),(2) & (3))

CHAPTER 30

1. d   (2C:30-2a.)
2. e   (2C:30-6)
3. b   (2C:30-6b.(3))
4. b   (2C:30-4a.)
5. d   (2C:30-7a.)
6. e   (2C:30-7b.)
7. c   (2C:30-6a.)
8. e   (2C:30-2, 2C:27-1g.)

CHAPTER 33

1. c   (2C:33-4b.)
2. e   (2C:12-3b.)

3. d   (2C:33-4e.)
4. b   (2C:33-9)
5. b   (2C:33-9)
6. b   (2C:33-1a.)
7. c   (2C:33-2.1d.)
8. a   (2C:33-2a.)
9. e   (2C:33-4a.)
10. d   (2C:33-12a., b., & c.)
11. b   (2C:33-13)
12. e   (2C:33-14)
13. d   (2C:33-16)
14. b   (2C:33-20)
15. a   (2C:33-26)
16. e   (2C:33-27)
17. b   (2C:33-3a.)
18. a   (2C:33-2a. & b.)
19. e   (2C:33-1b.)
20. b   (2C:33-8)
21. d   (2C:33-2)

CHAPTER 34

1. a   (2C:34-3b.)
2. d   (2C:34-3e.(1))
3. e   (2C:34-1c.(1) &
        2C:34-1b.(3) & (4))
4. e   (2C:34-1b.(3))
5. c   (2C:34-1c.(4),
        2C:34-1b.(1))
6. c   (2C: 34-1c.(4),
        2C:34-1b.(1))
7. b   (2C:34-1c.(2),
        2C:34-1b.(7))
8. d   (2C:34-2b.)

9. e   (2C:34-5b.)
10. b   (2C:34-1c.(3),
        2C:34-1b.(2),
        2C:34-1a.(4)(a),
        2C:34-1a.(4)(c))
11. e   (2C:34-1)
12. a   (2C:34-1)

CHAPTER 35

1. b   (2C:35-5b.(1)
2. c   (2C:35-4.1c.)
3. a   (2C:35-4.1a. & b.)
4. d   (2C:35-5b.(1))
5. a   (2C:35-7)
6. b   (2C:35-7.1a. & b.)
7. c   (2C:35-7.1a., 2C:35-
        5a.(1), 2C:35-5b.(2))
8. e   (2C:35-5b.(10)(a)
9. d   (2C:35-5b.(6))
10. b   (2C:35-5b.(1))
11. d   (2C:35-9a.,
        2C:35-9b.(2)(a))
12. c   (2C:35-11a.(1), 2C:35-
        11d.,2C:35-5a.(2))
13. d   (2C:35-10a.(4))
14. e   (2C:35-11)

CHAPTER 36

1. e   (2C:36-2)
2. c   (2C:36-2)
3. b   (2C:36-5)
4. e   (2C:36-6)

CHAPTER 37

1. e (2C:37-2c.)
2. d (2C:37-2a.(1) & b.(2))
3. e (2C:37-2a.)
4. a (2C:37-4a.)
5. e (2C:37-4a.)
6. d (2C:37-3c.(1) & (2))
7. c (2C:37-7b.)

CHAPTER 38

1. e (2C:38-2c.)
2. c (2C:38-2a.(3))
3. d (2C:38-3b.)
4. d (2C:38-3a., 2C:38-3c.(2)(c),2C:38-3c.(4))
5. d (2C:38-4a.(1) & (2), 2C:38-4b.)

CHAPTER 39

1. c (2C:39-9.2)
2. e (2C:39-5d., 2C:39-4d.)
3. a (2C:39-4a.)
4. c (2C:15-1a.(2), 2C:15-1b.,2C:18-2a.(1), 2C:39-4a., 2C:39-7b., 2C:39-1r. & t.)
5. a (2C:15-1b., 2C:11-1c.)
6. d (2C:39-10a.(2))
7. d (2C:39-10b., 2C:58-8)

8. e (2C:39-5b., 2C:39-4.1)
9. d (2C:39-4d., 2C:39-3e.)
10. d (2C:39-3c., f, & h)
11. e (2C:39-3g.(1), 2C:39-6a.(1))
12. d (2C:39-16)

CHAPTER 40

1. c (2C:40-3a.,2C:2-10b.(1) 2C:12-1a.(3))
2. a (2C:12-1b.(1), 2C:2-10b., 2C:40-3b.)
3. b (2C:40-17)
4. c (2C:40-18a.)
5. c (2C:40-22)

CHAPTER 40A

1. d (2C:40A-4a., d.,& g.)
2. c (2C:40A-3)
3. c (2C:40A-1)

CHAPTER 41

1. d (2C:41-3a.)
2. b (2C:41-1a.)
3. d (2C:41-1d.(1) & (2), 2C:41-2a.)
4. d (2C:41-2a.)